Character in Crisis

Edited by J. H. Hexter

Spirit Versus Structure

Spirit Versus Structure

*Luther
and the
Institutions of the Church*

Jaroslav Pelikan

1817

*HARPER & ROW, PUBLISHERS
NEW YORK, EVANSTON, and LONDON*

Venované
Slovenskej Evanjelickej
Bohosloveckej Fakulte
v Bratislave

Dedicated to
The Slovak Evangelical
Theological Faculty
in Bratislava

Contents

Preface

THE COMMEMORATION of Luther's posting of the ninety-five theses, 450 years ago today, comes at a time when both the Roman Catholicism against which he protested and the Protestantism which he created are engaged in a profound examination of the question of "spirit *versus* structure." The definition of Christian character and the very meaning of Christian faith are fundamentally affected by its outcome. Both the vigor of the questions and the ambiguity of the answers in Luther's Reformation therefore seem relevant to the contemporary crisis in Christian institutions.

Instead of ransacking the works of Luther for his "ideas" about church structure, I have concentrated on the specific situations in which he himself was involved and therefore on the specific treatises addressed to those situations—in most instances, the only treatise he addressed to each situation. Each chapter, therefore, is essentially a "one-source" discussion. While I was writing this book, I "planted" in various symposia more fully documented discussions of its various themes; in the first footnote to each chapter I have referred to those discussions, to whose publishers I am grateful for permission to include some of the material here. As the dedication of the book makes clear, I am grateful also to my hosts in Bratislava, Czechoslovakia, where I delivered much of this material in a series of lectures in May 1967. In addition, I presented them to the Christian Theological Academy in Warsaw, also in that month. A little earlier, I gave three of these chapters under the auspices of the Portland (Oregon) Christian Lectureship, on April 26–27.

My thanks belong not only to these various hosts, but also to my secretary and editorial assistant, Mrs. Margaret Schulze, for her help in typing and retyping the manuscript. I should add, however, that the decisions about whether to capitalize the "s" in "spirit" (a problem of special complexity for English usage, as is the problem of whether to say "he" or "it" even for the Holy Spirit) were necessarily my own.

JAROSLAV PELIKAN

Yale University
October 31, 1967

Prologue: Character in Crisis

MARTIN LUTHER began the study of law in the spring of 1505—and in 1520 he threw the *Canon Law* into a bonfire. Also in 1505 he entered the Augustinian monastery at Erfurt—and in 1520 he declared that "few, if any, monasteries are really Christian in our day." He was ordained a priest of the Roman Catholic Church in 1507—and by 1520 he was virtually convinced that the pope of Rome was the Antichrist.[1]

This volume is a study of that "great renunciation." It is an exposition of the character and thought of Martin Luther, and at the same time an examination of the crisis of Christian institutions brought on by his Reformation. Of course, it is artificial to distinguish between character and thought, and especially artificial in Luther's case. Thus one of the best older biographies of him in English, that of Preserved Smith, proposed to deal chiefly with his "character," by contrast with earlier biographies, most of them in German, which had been preoccupied with his "theology."[2] Yet even Smith, despite his bias, had to devote most of his book to Luther's thought. For the career of Martin Luther was the career of his beliefs, his words were his principal deeds, and it was his ideas that had the consequences. On the other

1

hand, the ideas were always deeply rooted in Luther's own character and experience, apart from which they do not make much sense.

Two imposing schools of thought about human behavior, the Marxist and the Freudian, have recently applied their theories to the study of the crisis of the Reformation and of the character of Luther in that crisis. Having outgrown the crudities of an earlier generation of economic determinists, present-day Marxist scholars in Eastern Germany and the Slavic lands are diagnosing the crisis of Christian institutions during the sixteenth century in the light of the great historic conflicts in which the Reformation was caught up, particularly, of course, the clash between feudalism and the emerging new order. It is still too early to predict with confidence where the discussion of Western scholars with Marxist historiography will lead, but no serious student of the Reformation can afford to ignore it. At the same time, Marxist scholars have been finding out that the stereotypes of Friedrich Engels' monograph on *The Peasant War* are not adequate as a guide to the character of Luther, whose handling of this crisis and of the other crises of the Reformation is far too complex to admit of a simplistic explanation.[3] The Freudian understanding of the hidden motivations underlying human conduct has helped to produce, in a volume of analysis by Erik Erikson and then in a play by John Osborne, a moving portrayal of Luther's rebellion against constituted authority. Oversimplified though it is to reduce the crisis of Luther's Reformation to his conflict with his father, the Freudian explanation of Luther's character, like the Marxist explanation of the historical crisis, does show again that no single hypothesis can account for the stand of this character in this crisis.[4]

Both hypotheses, moreover, seem to ignore the subtler relations between the character and the crisis: Luther did not renounce only the massive structures that stood as authorities over him (such as the papacy) or as traditions behind him (such as the councils of the church). Luther's Reformation was a crisis of the very structures in which he himself, as a man and a Christian and a priest, was fundamentally and personally involved: the ordained priesthood, monasticism, the practice of infant baptism, the canon law, and the sacramental system. Underlying the crisis of these five structures in Luther's Reformation is his understanding of the tension between spirit and structure. Obviously it is arbitrary to select 1520, as we have done above (or any other year, for that matter) as *the* date for Luther's declaration of independence from the structures of institutional Catholicism. Yet in the judgment both of his contemporaries and of later historians, Luther's declaration of independence is sounded most boldly and most radically in his treatise of 1520 on *The Babylonian Captivity of the Church*. Our exposition of spirit *versus* structure begins, then, with his treatment of that tension in *The Babylonian Captivity,* as much as possible in his own words.

But the problem of spirit *versus* structure is not dismissed so easily as all that. After Luther had issued his declaration of independence and had launched his movement, it fell to his lot to confront each of these structures again, this time in the context of his new responsibilities. It was one thing to defy structures in the name of the spirit; it was quite another to cope with the concrete need for structures. We shall therefore follow our examination of spirit *versus* structure in *The Babylonian Captivity* with a study of how Luther dealt with each of these structures head on in crisis, and again we shall use his own words from his chief writings on the specific crisis. Both the crisis of the Reformation and the character of Martin Luther should be illuminated by such a study.

1

Spirit *Versus* Structure (1520)

THE INSTITUTIONS of medieval Christendom were in trouble, and everyone knew it. Intended as windows through which men might catch a glimpse of the Eternal, they had become opaque, so that the faithful looked at them rather than through them. The structures of the church were supposed to act as vehicles for the spirit— both for the Spirit of God and for the spirit of man. Here the Christian believer was to find, in an available and indeed palpable form, the very grace of God. Instead, what he found was a distortion of the faith, a relapse into unbelief and immorality—in fact, a whole series of obstacles to the authentic life of the human spirit and to the activity of the Holy Spirit. Captive in ecclesiastical structures that no longer served as channels of divine life and means of divine grace, the spiritual power of the Christian gospel pressed to be released.

The pressure exploded in the Reformation. When Luther denounced the structures of institutional Catholicism, he was a traitor to his class. As an Augustinian friar and a priest, as a doctor of divinity and a university professor, as a "young man on the way up" who was already being mentioned as an obvious candidate for ecclesiastical preferment, he had everything to lose and nothing to gain by his defection. His friends and his enemies agreed that he was jeopardizing his career. But Luther was the kind of man to whom character was more important than career, one who felt obliged to obey God rather than man even if this meant breaking with the establishment. One by one, the structures of the church were thrust into the glare of the word of God and forced to show their true colors. It was part of Luther's character, as we shall see in this chapter, that while he was engaged in such an analysis he appeared to be heedless of consequences. If a structure hallowed by usage and supported by authority did not stand up under the analysis, that was simply too bad for the structure. But it was also part of Luther's character, as we shall see in subsequent chapters, that both his own convictions and the press of outer circumstances forced him to look again at the very structures he had attacked. Thus the tension between spirit and structure was fundamental to Luther's Reformation, as he made clear when he announced his programmatic demands in *The Babylonian Captivity of the Church*.[1]

SPIRIT VERSUS STRUCTURE

It is interesting to note that while Luther, as could be expected, made frequent use of the term "spirit" in *The Babylonian Captivity,* he also employed the term "structure" a couple of times, and on both occasions in a negative sense. Summarizing the arguments of his opponent, Augustin von Alfeld, Luther commented sarcastically: "This he lays down as his 'infallible foundation' of a structure so worthy of the holy and heavenly 'observance.'" And a little later, in a critique of the theory of transubstantiation, he declared that Aristotle's use of the terms "substance" and "accident" diverged from that of Thomas Aquinas, so that "this great man is to be pitied for . . . building an unfortunate structure upon an unfortunate foundation."[2] In both instances Luther appears to have been using the word "structure" to refer to theological arguments and to their literary formulation, rather than to the institutions of the church being defended in those arguments. Thus he followed the sense of the word suggested by Seneca's phrase, "the properties of words . . . both the structure and the argumentation," rather than that implied in Westcott's statement that "Christianity . . . is not a structure of institutions."[3] But Luther's treatment of the issue of "spirit *versus* structure" was not confined to his use of the actual term "structure."

His use of the term "spirit" and its derivatives was considerably more relevant to the issue. He attacked his opponents for making the claim "that what is decreed by the church is of no less authority than what is decreed by God, since the church is under the guidance of the Holy Spirit." Luther was willing to acknowledge the presence of a "mind in the church, when under the enlightenment of the Spirit she judges and approves doctrines; she is unable to prove it, and yet is most certain of having it." But this acknowledgment did not mean that the Spirit and the structure were to be identified, or that the institutional church could claim these prerogatives for its decrees about such things as sacraments in a simple and automatic way. "For who knows which is the church that has the Spirit? For when such decisions are made, there are usually only a few bishops or scholars present."[4] The structures of the institutional church, such as church councils, could err; for they were not entitled to claim for themselves an authority over that possession of the Spirit which, as a possession *by* the Spirit, had been promised to the church.

Therefore the equation of spirit and structure was an injustice to both. Luther saw it as an attempt to limit the working of the Spirit and to usurp for the structures of the church an authority over the Spirit to which they were not entitled. But he also attacked it for removing from those structures the very power of the Spirit which had been promised to them. One target of this attack was the twelfth-century theologian, Peter Lombard, together with the later scholastics who had commented on his *Sentences*. Just ten years earlier, in 1510, Luther himself had, as a fledgling professor, lectured on the *Sentences* of Peter Lombard and was therefore a "Sententiary." But now in 1520 he denounced the Sententiaries because "at their best [they] write only of the 'matter' and 'form' of the sacraments; that is, they treat of the dead and death-dealing letter of the sacraments, but leave untouched the spirit, life, and use, that is, the truth of the divine promise and our faith." Spirit there was, or at any rate could be, in the structures of the church; but when the distinction between spirit and structure was blurred, as it had been both by medieval prelates and by medieval theologians, those very structures were crushed by a literalism that was death-dealing as well as dead. This "worthless religion of this age of ours, the most godless and thankless of all ages" paid more attention to the ritual trifles of human invention than to the commands and promises of divine institution. Thus "our theologians never taught us" an awareness of the gifts granted to the church and of the use to which these gifts ought to be put. "For if we are instructed with this judgment of the Spirit, we shall not mistakenly rely on those things which are wrong."[5] It was to this "judgment of the Spirit" rather than to the theories of the theologians that Luther wanted the church to look for guidance and instruction.

Where the judgment of the Spirit was ignored, the result was not only that claims were made for ecclesiastical structures which were appropriate only to the Spirit, but also that the spontaneous creations of the Spirit were by legislation made a part of the structure. An outstanding example, of which we shall be speaking in greater detail both here and in Chapter 3, were the vows of the monks. Far from denying out of hand either the sincerity of such vows or the authenticity of the vocation to them, Luther recognized them as extraordinary phenomena in the Christian life. "Certain works are wrought by the Spirit in a few men, but they must not be made an example or a mode of life for all." Precisely because the Spirit had to have the freedom to call forth such heroic works when and where he pleased, it was wrong to reverse the priority of Spirit over structure and to make an "example or a mode of life," that is, an ecclesiastical structure, of this free activity of the Spirit in the Christian life. Indeed, it was wrong to reverse the priority of Spirit over structure even in the case of those structures which were not invented by men, but instituted by God. Significantly, both baptism and the eucharist are examined in *The Babylonian Captivity* for their "spiritual" rather than

merely for their sacramental function. When the apostle
Paul spoke of death and resurrection in baptism, Luther
insisted, this was not to be taken as a "false sign," as
though the statements of the apostle were to be "under-
stood only allegorically as the death of sin and the life
of grace, as many understand it, but as actual death and
resurrection." This referred to faith, so that "faith is
truly a death and a resurrection, that is, it is that spiritual baptism into which we are submerged and from
which we rise." For contrary to the opinions of the ritual-
ists, faith "makes us free in spirit from all those scruples
and fancies."[6]

Even more explicit and detailed was the application of
the term "spiritual" to the eucharist. As "faith is truly
that spiritual baptism," so also "no eating can give life
except that which is by faith. For that is truly a spiritual
and living eating. . . . The sacramental eating does not
give life." The formula of Augustine, "Believe, and you
have eaten," which was quoted frequently in the writings
of the reformers, provided the support of tradition for
this emphasis upon faith as the true eating. When Luther's opponents quoted the discourses in the sixth chapter of St. John in support of their view of the eucharist,
he replied that this chapter "does not refer to the sacrament in a single syllable," but that Christ "was speaking
of a spiritual eating." Later in the treatise, "Believe,
and you have eaten" once more provided the occasion
for Luther's consideration of "spiritual eating." He dis-
tinguished between "word" and "sign" in the sacraments and therefore between "testament" and "sacrament," and, as could be expected, he gave "word"
priority over "sign" and "testament" priority over "sac-

rament." This brought him to the radical conclusion: "Therefore I can hold mass every day, indeed, every hour, for I can set the words of Christ before me and with them feed and strengthen my faith as often as I choose. This is a truly spiritual eating and drinking."[7] The constant refrain of "spirit," "spiritual," and "spiritually" in these declarations makes it abundantly clear that Luther wanted to elevate spirit over structure, in opposition to an identification of spirit and structure. "To such an extent," he exclaimed, "has 'ecclesiastical' today come to mean the same as 'spiritual'!"[8]

PRIESTHOOD AND MINISTRY

Because "ecclesiastical" had come to mean the same as "spiritual" and structure and spirit were being identified, it was inevitable that the clergy would "imagine themselves to be the church . . . the 'spiritual estate' . . . when they are anything but that." Not only from his theological studies, but from his own experience of fifteen years as a monk and a priest, Luther knew very well that the structure of the ordained priesthood, with its sacramental functions and indelible character, was indispensable to the entire institutional structure of the church, so that "if this sacrament [ordination] and this fiction ever fall to the ground, the papacy with its 'characters' will scarcely survive. Then our joyous liberty will be restored to us." This whole structure was, therefore, a "yoke of tyranny." Especially onerous was the tyranny of the ordained clergy over the laity, which exalted ordination by the ecclesiastical structure over ordination by the Holy Spirit; "trusting in the external anointing

. . . they exalt themselves above the rest of the lay Christians, who are only anointed with the Holy Spirit." Once again it was the identification of spirit with structure that lay at the heart of the problem. The command in Matt. 18:17, "Tell it to the church," was taken to mean, "as these babblers interpret it, to the prelate or priest."[9]

The equation of the spiritual with the ecclesiastical and of the ecclesiastical with the institutional meant that the position of the clergy was interpreted chiefly in a juridical and administrative way. As in the sacramental system the sign had been elevated over faith and the sacrament over the testament, so here faith had been subordinated to juridical authority and the laity to the clergy. Luther summarized the contrast in an epigram: "They say nothing of faith which is the salvation of the people, but babble only of the despotic power of the pontiffs, whereas Christ says nothing at all of power, but speaks only of faith." Faith was the anointing with the Holy Spirit, but they made everything dependent on the "external anointing" of the priest. The founding of the church by Christ and the instituting of the apostolic ministry were interpreted as the establishment of a legal institution and the designation of its powers and prerogatives. But "Christ has not ordained authorities or powers or lordships in his church, but ministries."[10] The "despotic power" of the clergy over the laity was a perversion of the institution of Christ both because it deprived the laity of their own priestly rights and because it substituted juridical authority for ministry in the clergy.

Thus the command, "Tell it to the church," did not mean, "to the prelate or priest"; for the context made it clear that "this is said to each and every Christian." Not the position of a man in the institutional structure but his relation to the Holy Spirit was what made him a priest. Hence every Christian was "anointed and sanctified both in body and soul with the oil of the Holy Spirit," regardless of whether or not he had received the chrism administered by a prelate. In 1523, as Chapter 2 will point out, Luther developed a theory which appeared to make the doctrine of the ministry dependent on the doctrine of the priesthood of believers. But already here in 1520 he declared: "If they were forced to grant that all of us that have been baptized are equally priests, as indeed we are, and that only the ministry was committed to them, yet with our common consent, they would then know that they have no right to rule over us except insofar as we freely concede it." But the order of priority had been reversed here, too, so that the true priests were regarded as mere laymen while those who called themselves priests did not perform their priestly functions. Baptism, then, was the sacrament of priesthood; ordination was merely the assignment of certain public responsibilities. "Let everyone, therefore, who knows himself to be a Christian, be assured of this, that we are all equally priests, that is to say, we have the same power in respect to the word and the sacraments."[11]

Having said this, however, Luther went on in the very next sentence to clarify it: "However, no one may make use of this power except by the consent of the community or by the call of a superior. (For what is the common property of all, no individual may arrogate to himself, unless he is called.) And therefore this 'sacrament' of ordination, if it is anything at all, is nothing else than a certain rite by which one is called to the ministry of the church." The key word here was "ministry." As Luther had said a little earlier, "only the ministry was committed to them [the ordained], yet with our common consent." On this issue, therefore, the contrast between spirit and structure took the form of a contrast between ministry and power. In the words by which Jesus instituted baptism, "there was no conferring of any power . . . but only the instituting of the ministry of those who baptize." Similarly, in the words by which he instituted baptism, "there was no conferring of any power but only of the ministry of the one who absolves." And in the words by which he instituted the eucharist, "nothing is said of power, but only of the ministry." Yet the same subordination of spirit to structure which had robbed the laity of their priesthood had also robbed the clergy of their ministry. "As the priests are, so let their ministry and duty be. For a bishop who does not preach the gospel or practice the cure of souls—what is he but an idol in the world, who has nothing but the name and appearance of a bishop?"[12] The laity, the true priests, had become mere subjects under the tyranny of the clergy; the clergy, who were supposed to be ministers, called themselves the priests. Just what this radical theory implied for Luther's practical recommendations about the structures of the church when an emergency arose, we shall see in the next chapter.

MONASTICISM

Among the clergy, a special place was occupied by the members of the religious orders. Luther was, after all, both an Augustinian monk and a priest. The contrast between renewal of structure and renewal by the Spirit is especially evident in his treatment of monasticism. Early in the treatise on *The Babylonian Captivity* Luther recognized that a consistent application of the position he was voicing about the proper relation between spirit and structure would lead to a drastic reorientation of ecclesiastical life, including the life of the religious orders. "But you will say: What is this? Will you not overturn the practice and teaching of all the churches and monasteries, by virtue of which they have flourished all these centuries?" Luther's response reflected his bravado, but something beyond bravado as well: "This is the very thing that has constrained me to write of the captivity of the church. . . . What do I care about the number and influence of those who are in this error? The truth is mightier than all of them."[13]

As we have noted earlier, Luther was not indifferent to the special gifts and vocation of the Holy Spirit by which men were called to become heroes of religious faith; nor did he wish to quench that Spirit. His very defense of spirit against structure obliged him to recognize that "certain works are wrought by the Spirit in a few men," but the same defense also forced him to warn that such works "must not be made an example or a mode of life for all." Yet because it was the Holy Spirit who worked such extraordinary deeds in the heroes of God, the attempt to create an administrative structure of monastic rules and lifelong vows was, by definition, doomed to fail. For it was the paradox of Christian heroism that "no vow will ever become binding and valid until we have become spiritual, and no longer have any need of vows." Consequently vows became possible only when they were no longer necessary. From this it followed as pastoral wisdom that it would be best "to keep such lofty modes of living free of vows, and leave them to the Spirit alone as they were of old, and never in any way change them into a mode of life which is perpetually binding."[14] Since they were a matter of the spirit, indeed of the Holy Spirit, monastic vows should not be made a matter of the administrative structures and juridical authority of the church.

This still left, of course, those structures that had already been created by monastic vows and religious orders, the structures upon which, in fact, most of the church's ministry in the areas of missions, welfare, and education had depended. In his treatment of those structures Luther felt able to "set forth publicly the counsel I have learned under the Spirit's guidance." He was "speaking now in behalf of the church's liberty and the glory of baptism." Therefore his evaluation of monastic vows was set into that framework. His counsel was, quite simply and emphatically, "that all vows should be completely abolished and avoided, whether of religious orders, or about pilgrimages or about any works whatsoever, that we may remain in that which is supremely religious and most rich in works—the freedom of baptism." Those who exercised authority over the structures of the church should, therefore, "abolish all those vows and religious orders, or at least not . . . approve them." Lacking so radical a decision by those in authority, Christians should "abstain from all vows, above all from the major and lifelong vows." But if none of this counsel proved effective and the monastic vows and religious orders continued nevertheless, Luther was at least obliged to warn everyone against taking a vow or entering an order "unless he is forearmed with this knowledge and understands that the works of monks and priests, however holy and arduous they may be, do not differ one whit in the sight of God from the works of the rustic laborer in the field or the woman going about her household tasks, but that all works are measured before God by faith alone."[15] The proposal that an "intramundane asceticism," or a voluntary monasticism wrought by the extraordinary operation of the Holy Spirit, be substituted for the structures of the religious orders and their vows continued to play an important role in Luther's ethic. In Chapter 3 we shall examine what this proposal meant (or did not mean) for the concrete structures of missions, welfare, and education.

THE PROBLEM OF INFANT BAPTISM

Yet Luther had to recognize that as soon as he had made baptism rather than ordination the sacrament of authentic priesthood, he was only moving the question into another area that was, to say the least, equally controversial. For priesthood had to be a task consciously assumed and responsibly administered. No one could be a priest unless he could say that he had freely taken the priesthood upon himself. And as soon as Luther had made not only the priesthood but, in effect, all the structures of the church dependent upon a divine promise and upon human faith, he was creating a special problem for the traditional defense of infant baptism. Chapter 4 will describe how the challenge of the Anabaptists compelled Luther to explore the problem of

infant baptism in greater detail. But even before that
challenge he was obliged by his own polemics against the
elevation of structure over spirit to examine whether his
position implied that baptism should be restricted to
those who could have explicit faith.

He certainly seemed to be saying as much in his expo-
sitions of the doctrine of baptism in *The Babylonian
Captivity*. With emphasis he stated: "The first thing to
be considered about baptism is the divine promise, which
says: 'He who believes and is baptized will be saved.' "
But that promise required faith as its corollary, so that
Luther went on to say: "But we must so consider it as to
exercise our faith in it. . . . For unless faith is present
or is conferred in baptism, baptism will profit us nothing." The word of promise from God's side and the re-
ceiving faith from man's side were decisive in any sacrament, including baptism. It was not the sacramental
structure that saved, but faith and the promise. "Thus it
is not baptism that justifies or benefits anyone, but it is
faith in that word of promise to which baptism is added.
This faith justifies, and fulfils that which baptism signi-
fies." When the sacramental structure was emphasized
apart from faith, the entire significance of baptism was
distorted; and just this had happened in the church.
"Now faith is passed over in silence, and the church is
smothered with endless laws concerning works and ceremonies; the power and understanding of baptism are set
aside, and faith in Christ is obstructed." The centrality
of faith also connected baptism to the continuing life of
penance; not the structure of the penitential system, but
the life of the spirit was decisive, for "whatever we do
in this life which mortifies the flesh or quickens the spirit
has to do with our baptism."[16]

The more Luther emphasized spirit over structure in baptism and therefore assigned a central position to faith in the word of promise, the more problematical infant baptism seemed to become. For he had to admit that infants "do not comprehend the promise of God and cannot have the faith of baptism." Thus if, as he was arguing, "these two, promise and faith, must necessarily go together," infant baptism would appear to be illegitimate. The insistence on faith in the word of the promise and the acceptance of infant baptism appeared to be mutually incompatible: "Either faith is not necessary or else infant baptism is without effect." Within the context of the sacramental system against which Luther was protesting, a justification of infant baptism was possible on several grounds; but the most important of these was the very ground which Luther was attacking, namely, the efficacy inherent in the sacramental act itself. Even in his discussion of infant baptism, therefore, he had to insist that "the sacraments do what they do not by their own power, but by the power of faith, without which they do nothing at all."[17] With what seems so subjective an understanding of sacramental efficacy, what justification could be found for affirming the objective validity of infant baptism?

At least three traditional arguments were presented here in *The Babylonian Captivity*. The one to which Luther resorted in response to his own objections about infant baptism was, as he put it, "what all say: Infants are aided by the faith of others, namely, those who bring them for baptism. For the word of God is powerful enough, when uttered, to change even a godless heart, which is no less unresponsive and helpless than any infant. So through the prayer of the believing church which presents it, a prayer to which all things are possible, the infant is changed, cleansed, and renewed by infused faith." A second argument turned the tables on the objection to infant baptism, saying, in effect, that the faith of adults was more problematical than the faith of infants. For God had "desired that by [baptism] little children, who were incapable of greed and superstition, might be initiated and sanctified in the simple faith of his word; even today baptism has its chief blessing for them." And Luther added: "If the intention had been to give this sacrament to adults and older people, I do not believe that it could possibly have retained its power and its glory against the tyranny of greed and superstition." The third argument was based on the objective structure of the ministerial office, which means that the formula "I baptize you," about which there had been controversy between East and West, could be paraphrased to read: "What I do, I do not by my own authority, but in the name and stead of God. . . . The Doer and the minister are different persons, but the work of both is the same work, or rather, it is the work of the Doer alone through my ministry."[18] As the crisis of the Reformation deepened, Luther had to go considerably beyond these arguments to justify the retention of infant baptism.

CHURCH LAW AND DIVINE LAW

Supporting all the other structures of the church, deriving their validation from these structures but in turn providing these structures with their sanction and support, were two overarching ecclesiastical institutions in which every Christian, but especially every priest, had to be deeply involved: the canon law and the sacramental system. Both of them claimed Luther's attention in *The Babylonian Captivity.*

Canon law was for Luther the supreme instance of the equation of spirit and structure. The words of Christ to Peter in Matt. 16:19 were taken as an authorization granting "the pope the power to make laws," even though Christ was speaking of something altogether different from "taking the whole church captive and oppressing it with laws." It would not do, therefore, to "flaunt the authority of the church and the power of the pope in my face," for "these do not annul the words of God and the testimony of the truth." The identification of spirit with structure had brought about an identification of church law with divine law, which meant that the supporters of the ecclesiastical institution "constantly exalt their own ordinances above the commands of God." They supposed that Christ had "left us the gospel so that the pontiffs might sound the voice of Christ," which they equated with "their own ordinances." The liberty of the sons of God had thus been exchanged for a new tyranny of laws, which, though enacted by men, were vested with the authority of the commandments of God; "and we serve in bondage instead of being free—we, to whom all days, places, persons, and all external things are one and the same." As a result, the church was under a tyranny more grim "than the synagogue or any other nation under heaven."[19]

The solution was to draw a radical distinction between the commandments of God and "those that have been invented by men in the church." It did not matter if "all the world holds and practices the contrary." For in op-

position to all the laws and ordinances of the church,
Luther was ready to cry out: "No law, whether of men
or of angels, may rightfully be imposed upon Christians without their consent, for we are free of all laws."
And again: "Neither pope nor bishop nor any other man
has the right to impose a single syllable of law upon a
Christian man; if he does, it is done in the spirit of
tyranny." Although the Hussites had been condemned
for their disobedience to the laws of the church, they
had "the word and act of Christ on their side"; for what
was being defended against them was a law ordained by
"the tyrants of the churches, without the consent of the
church, which is the people of God." Therefore not the
Hussites but "you Romans" were the true heretics and
schismatics, for presuming "upon your figments alone
against the clear Scriptures of God." Having delivered
himself of this complaint against the equation of the law
of the church with the law of God, Luther warned "the
pope and all his papists: Unless they will abolish their
laws and ordinances, and restore to Christ's churches
their liberty and have it taught among them, they are
guilty of all the souls that perish under this miserable
captivity, and the papacy is truly the kingdom of Babylon
and the very Antichrist."[20]

In a few places in *The Babylonian Captivity* Luther's
attack on canon law was sharpened to the point of an
attack on the capacity of law as such, of any law, to accomplish its ends; in other places, however, he spoke as
the defender of the principles of the law. The latter
theme was sounded, for example, when, near the beginning of the treatise, Luther warned of the possible consequences of withholding the chalice from the laity in

the administration of holy communion: "If we permit one institution of Christ to be changed, we make all of his laws invalid, and any man may make bold to say that he is not bound by any other law or institution of Christ." But the former theme was the more striking, also because of its contrast with what Luther taught about law generally. "No state," he said here in *The Babylonian Captivity,* "is governed successfully by means of laws. If the ruler is wise, he will govern better by a natural sense of justice than by laws. If he is not wise, he will foster nothing but evil by legislation, since he will not know what use to make of the laws nor how to adapt them to the case at hand." As an alternative Luther suggested that "if there is knowledge of the divine law combined with natural wisdom, then written laws will be entirely superfluous and harmful." "Above all," he concluded, "love needs no laws whatever." Applied to concrete moral and legal issues, this philosophy of law does not seem to have led to very specific conclusions. In the area of marriage and divorce, for example, Luther's observations on law and practice here in *The Babylonian Captivity* were quite inconclusive. It was consistent with the position just quoted when, contrasting divine law and church law, he asserted that "marriage itself, being a divine institution, is incomparably superior to any laws, so that marriage should not be annulled for the sake of the law, rather the laws should be broken for the sake of marriage." But he went on a little later to state a preference for bigamy over divorce, adding: "But whether it is allowable, I do not venture to decide." Nor would he permit the pope and bishops to decide; but "if two learned and good men agreed in the name of Christ and published their opinion in the spirit of Christ, I should prefer their judgment even to such [church] councils as are assembled nowadays." Again it was the spirit of Christ that was to be preferred to the structure of canon law. Indeed, marriage legislation was the best possible illustration of the corruption introduced by canon law, "so that there is no hope of betterment unless we abolish at one stroke all the laws of all men, and having restored the gospel of liberty we follow it in judging and regulating all things. Amen."[21]

THE SACRAMENTAL SYSTEM

One reason for the vehemence of Luther's opposition to the canon law was the authorization it seemed to provide for the sacramental system. He knew, for example, that his condemnations would "displease those who believe that the number and the use of the sacraments are to be learned not from the sacred Scriptures, but from the Roman see." Luther's elevation of spirit over structure, therefore, did not spare even the most fundamental structure of traditional Christian piety, the sacramental system. More than either dogma or the papacy, it was the sacramental system that constituted the heart of religious belief and practice for the true Christian. Luther's attack on the sacramental system, which occupied a large part of *The Babylonian Captivity,* was therefore an important measure of how radically he was willing to subordinate structure to spirit. "The invention of sacraments is of recent date," he was willing to say, thus denying the validity of the development of church structures out of which the sacramental system had emerged.

Not only did the church have no right to create or designate sacraments; even an apostle did not possess such authority. Therefore even if the epistle of James, with its command to anoint, were by an apostle, and even if that command implied a sacramental action (both of which Luther denied), "I would still say that no apostle has the right on his own authority to institute a sacrament, that is, to give a divine promise with a sign attached. For this belongs to Christ alone." Apostolic precedent was not a sufficient ground for designating some action as a sacrament; "If everything the apostles did is a sacrament, why have they not rather made preaching a sacrament?" Because the invention of sacraments was a recent thing, the very term "sacrament" was misleading. "Nowhere in all of the Holy Scriptures is this word *sacramentum* employed in the sense in which we use the term; it has an entirely different meaning. For wherever it occurs it denotes not the sign of a sacred thing, but the sacred, secret, hidden thing itself." And therefore the sacramental system was an elaborate complication of what was given in the word of God; in fact, "if I were to speak according to the usage of the Scriptures, I should have only one single sacrament, but with three sacramental signs."[22]

This "one sacrament" was the word of Christ, which was communicated through each of the "three sacramental signs." In the use of the sacraments, therefore, it was essential to "open our eyes and learn to pay heed more to the word than to the sign, more to faith than to the work or use of the sign." Only in this way, for example, was it possible to justify the way of life attributed to the desert fathers in the ancient church, who "did not receive the sacrament in any form for many years at a time." On this basis Luther found it possible to designate even a non-sacramental rite as a channel of grace and hence not to "deny that forgiveness and peace are granted through extreme unction; not because it is a sacrament divinely instituted, but because he who receives it believes that these blessings are granted to him. For the faith of the recipient does not err, however much the minister may err." If, then, the decisive factor was not whether a particular rite could in fact qualify as a sacrament, it would follow that "there are still a few other things which it might seem possible to regard as sacraments; namely, all those things to which a divine promise has been given, such as prayer, the word, and the cross." Nevertheless, Luther demurred at such a generalized application of the term "sacrament," preferring to affirm the historical development by which "it has seemed proper to restrict the name of sacrament to those promises which have signs attached to them." It was, therefore, much more than a prudential or a politic gesture when Luther assured his reader that "I do not say this because I condemn the seven sacraments, but because I deny that they can be proved from the Scriptures." The word had priority over the sacraments, be they two or three or seven in number, because in at least some sense the "sacramental signs" all were functions of the one "sacrament," which was Christ. It was, in fact, a general axiom which Luther enunciated: "What is true in regard to Christ is also true in regard to the sacraments."[23]

The sacramental system was wrong not only because it contained so-called sacraments that had been instituted by human rather than by divine authority, but also because even those sacraments for which there was divine authority had become vastly more complicated, both in their meaning and in their mode of observance, as a result of human tampering. "The more closely our mass resembles the first mass of all, which Christ performed at the Last Supper, the more Christian it will be. But Christ's mass was most simple, without any display." The most wicked of all the abuses connected with the mass, the "third captivity" in Luther's catalogue here, was the sacrificial interpretation of the eucharist, as a result of which all sorts of ritualistic elaboration and commercial exploitation had developed. In opposition to all this, Luther urged that "in the first place . . . we must be particularly careful to put aside whatever has been added to its original simple institution by the zeal and devotion of men. . . . We must turn our eyes and hearts simply to the institution of Christ and this alone." All else was a human invention, which added nothing to the word of Christ but only detracted from it. This primitivistic emphasis upon the simplicity of the original institution belonged to the demand that ecclesiastical structures, including liturgical forms, be subordinated to what was "spiritual" in the sacraments, that is, to the word; for although "all the endless ceremonies doubtless symbolize excellent things to be fulfilled in the spirit, yet, because there is no word of divine promise attached to these things, they can in no way be compared with the signs of baptism and the bread." Doctrinal elaborations, too, had to be subordinated to the true, spiritual meaning of the sacraments. Transubstantiation was bad philosophy, and worse theology, according to Luther, not because he rejected the real presence, but because he insisted on it. In this affirmation of the real presence combined with a rejection of transubstantiation, he was glad to join his position to that of the common people, who "as they do not understand, neither do they dispute whether accidents are present without substance, but believe with a simple faith that Christ's body and blood are truly contained there, and leave to those who have nothing else to do the argument about what contains them."[24]

The pastoral theme audible in this judgment is even more noticeable in Luther's treatment of private confession in *The Babylonian Captivity*. Luther was well aware of the abuses to which private confession was subject; it had, after all, been such an abuse that had called forth the ninety-five theses of 1517. He was speaking as a priest who had responsibility for the administration of the sacrament of penance when he expressed his regret "that we absolve sinners before the satisfaction has been completed, so that they are more concerned about completing the satisfaction . . . than they are about contrition," viz., more concerned about meeting the demands of an ecclesiastical structure (the prescription of certain satisfactions) than about obeying the spirit of a divine command (the call to contrition and repentance). He also knew, again from personal experience as a priest, not only "that contrition has been exposed to tyranny and avarice," but especially that "it is confession and satisfaction that have become the chief workshops of greed and power" and the sources of financial gain. Within the very argument of *The Babylonian Captivity* Luther took both sides of the question on the sacramental nature of penance. At the beginning of the treatise he proposed "for the present [to] maintain that there are but three [sacraments] : baptism, penance, and the bread." But by the time he had finished the treatise, he questioned whether penance could truly be called a sacrament, since it "lacks the divinely instituted visible sign, and is . . . nothing but a way and a return to baptism." None of this detracted in any way, however, from the worth of penance, especially of private confession. "I am," Luther said, "heartily in favor of it, even though it cannot be proved from the Scriptures. It is useful, even necessary, and I would not have it abolished. Indeed, I rejoice that it exists in the church of Christ, for it is a cure without equal for distressed consciences."[25] The structure of private confession, then, was to be retained as an aid and a cure for the spirit.

Luther's ambivalence about the sacramental nature of penance is based on the long-standing difficulty of defining what constituted a sacrament. Over the years of his polemics against the sacramental system, Luther devoted very little of his attack to the standard scholastic definitions, recognizing that any definition must be arbitrary. But on one aspect of the definition he was insistent: "To constitute a sacrament there must be above all things else a word of divine promise, by which faith may be exercised." Therefore "the mass is nothing else than the divine promise or testament of Christ." From this emphasis upon the promise in the sacraments it followed as a corollary that faith was required. "These two, promise and faith, must necessarily go together. For without the promise there is nothing to be believed; while without faith the promise is useless, since it is established and

fulfilled through faith. . . . Without this faith, whatever else is brought to [the mass] by way of prayers,
preparations, works, signs, or gestures is an incitement
to impiety rather than an exercise of piety." There were
many masses in the world, but very little attention to
faith in "the promises and riches that are offered to us."
In fact, the principal difference between the sacraments
of the Old Testament and those of the New was not "in
the effectiveness of their signs," but rather in this, that
the sacraments of the Old Testament "did not have attached to them any word of promise requiring faith,"
while those of the New Testament "have attached to
them a word of promise which requires faith, and they
cannot be fulfilled by any other work."[26] Attention to
the signs more than to the things signified, to the sacramental action more than to the promise and faith, was
the application to the sacramental system of the identification of spirit and structure; but structure was put in its
place when faith and the promise were made normative
for the sacraments. As Chapter 6 will document, the relation between faith and the promise continued to be the
key to Luther's attitude toward the sacramental system.

The ordained priesthood, the monastic orders, infant
baptism, canon law, the sacramental system—each of
these historic institutions was an integral element of the
one holy catholic and apostolic church as men had known
it and believed in it for more than a millennium. But
every one of these structures of catholic Christendom
was, in one way or another, now faced with a crisis as
a result of Luther's Reformation. Every one of these
structures had also been a constituent of Luther's own
personal faith and career. And so each of them de-

manded the attention of Luther the churchman as the Reformation took up the task of reorganizing the ecclesiastical life of Christian Europe in accordance with its principles. Having leveled these attacks at the very structures of the church upon which his own religious life had been founded, Luther had to address himself to each of them again in specific situations and with specific recommendations. That is to say, he had to come to terms with the necessity either of renewing the given structures or of creating new structures, which would, of course, inevitably be in need of eventual renewal. No trial oppressed Luther's spirit more often in his later years than this recognition that structure was inevitable, combined as the recognition was with a candid awareness that the institutions now being erected were not necessarily superior to those which had (often against Luther's advice) been swept away. In this institutional crisis the complexity of Luther's character became evident. We turn now to the five structures analyzed in *The Babylonian Captivity of the Church* and trace their fate in Luther's Reformation.

2

Priesthood and Ministry (1523)

DURING the quarter-century that followed the publication of *The Babylonian Captivity of the Church* in 1520, what had begun as a struggle in one man's soul became a crisis affecting all of catholic Christendom; a movement that originated within the Roman Catholic Church now became "a church" unto itself, in fact, an entire series of churches. Viewed from the perspective of *The Babylonian Captivity,* this development raises the question: Did the elevation of spirit over structure in this treatise contain within itself the institution-building power necessary for the establishment and maintenance of a proper ministry? Or could these new churches perhaps dispense with institutional life and become communities of the Holy Spirit in which the only structure was the free exercise of the universal priesthood of all believers?

That question became an insistent one far sooner than Luther had anticipated. It was not within the German lands that it first came to a head; for here the reformation of the churches in a given principality was carried out under the aegis of the ruling prince, so that at least some continuity of the ministry was preserved. If we turn to Luther for a consideration of the issue of ministerial continuity, we find surprisingly few instances where he both dealt with a practical problem of church structures and enunciated a theory to meet it. For example, Luther provided very little theological legitimation for the action of his colleague, John Bugenhagen, who ordained seven Lutheran bishops in Copenhagen without bothering to establish the continuity of their office through the apostolic succession of bishops. The visitation of the churches in Saxony in the late 1520's was carried out without a full-blown theological rationale, as can be seen from the designation of the princes as "emergency bishops." On the other hand, Luther's brief treatise of 1523, *On the Right and Power of a Christian Congregation or Community to Judge All Doctrine and to Call, Install, and Depose Ministers,* contented itself with brief comments on some of the most important biblical texts involved in this issue, without supplying practical instructions about how such calling, installing, and deposing were to be carried out within the structures of the institutional church.[1]

"CONCERNING THE MINISTRY"

In the same year, however, another writing was published under Luther's name, which provided specific instructions at least for the calling and installing, if not for the deposing, of ministers, as well as a detailed rationale for the continuity of the ministry of the church. This was the treatise *Concerning the Ministry,* which seems to have appeared in November 1523. It was called forth by the dire straits into which the Czech Utraquists, followers of John Hus, had come over the need for a continuity of church structure. The archbishopric of Prague had been vacant since 1421. From 1482 Augustin Lucian de Bessariis, bishop from the island of Santorino, had been in Bohemia ordaining Utraquist priests; but he had died in 1493, and the consistory of the Utraquist church had to find other devices for having its candidates for the priesthood validly ordained. The practice developed of sending such candidates elsewhere; for example, John Bechynka had been ordained in 1499 by the Armenian bishop in Lvov, and many others went to Italy to receive holy orders. Upon his return to Bohemia the newly ordained priest would have to renounce his promise not to administer the chalice to the laity at communion. The shortage of priests also made the Utraquists the victims of vagabond priests, who had been forced to leave Germany or Poland but found refuge in Bohemia; a German proverb, quoted by Luther, observed that anyone who in Germany deserved the gallows or the rack could be a priest among the Czechs.[2]

Taking advantage of this confused situation to advance his own ambitions, Havel [Gallus] Cahera Zatecky, who was pastor in Litomerice, managed to maneuver Luther into the position of supporting his candidacy for higher office. During the summer of 1523 Cahera was in Wittenberg, where he described the plight of the Utraquist church to Luther and sought his aid and counsel. This Luther provided in *Concerning the Ministry*, which, as we shall note in more detail a little later, contained an endorsement of Cahera as candidate for bishop. Armed with Luther's treatise, Cahera returned to Prague, and on August 24, 1523, he was elected as

one of the four administrators of the Utraquist consistory and assigned to the Tyn church. His subsequent
career need not detain us here, except to note that he
eventually betrayed Luther's confidence by surrendering
the Utraquist cause. "Hardly ever was Luther as disappointed in his hopes" as he was in Cahera.[3]

Basic to Luther's argument in *Concerning the Ministry* was the conviction that the method being used by
the Utraquists to assure continuity of church structure
was wrong. It was "chaos" and "Babylonian confusion,"
and Bohemia had become practically a "mendicant." If
this was the only way to obtain clergy, it would be far
better to dispense with an ordered ministry altogether
and to allow the head of the household to read the Bible
to his family and to baptize, even if this meant that they
would have to do without the eucharist for the rest of
their lives. It is a significant commentary on Luther's understanding of the structures of the church, however,
that while his denunciation of the Utraquist practice referred to their being forced to buy their ordination, it
did not mention the implications of simony for the validity of ordination, as this was set down in canon law and
was being discussed in his own time, for example, by
Pope Julius II. It concentrated, rather, on the disorder
this practice caused and on the "violation of conscience,
so that not a single one of you can ever rejoice in good
conscience that you have entered the sheep-fold by the
door [John 10:1]." Opinions might differ about the
right way of providing the structure of the ministry, and
some might be overly scrupulous and weak, i.e., too un-
sure of themselves to follow the way Luther was about

to recommend; but whatever might be the right way, the practice of the Utraquists was undoubtedly the wrong way.[4]

LUTHER'S RECOMMENDATIONS

If necessary, then, the Utraquists could live as had the Jews in exile, who, "upheld in their faith alone by the word of God . . . passed their lives among enemies while yearning for Jerusalem." But this was not necessary, for a continuity of the ministry could be provided. They should pray, individually and collectively, for the gift of the Holy Spirit. Then all those whose hearts had been touched by God to think and believe in harmony should meet and elect "one or more whom you desire." Through the laying on of hands by those who were "leaders among you" (presumably, though not unquestionably, referring to the political leaders of the Utraquist estates), these candidates were to be certified to the people and to the community as their new "bishops, ministers, or pastors." Eventually, Luther hoped, this procedure could lead to a restoration of true continuity of order, to a "rightful and evangelical archbishopric," as those who had been elected through this "free and apostolic rite" in turn elected one or more as their supervisors who would hold visitations among them.[5] And so a proper and legitimate ministry could be erected without recourse either to the morally questionable expedient of sending candidates elsewhere or to the expedient of accepting morally questionable priests simply because they happened to be episcopally ordained.

At the same time, Luther acknowledged—and Cahera

apparently expected him to acknowledge—that some of the Utraquists might be reluctant to adopt such a radical form of church structure and might prefer an order whose continuity with established succession could be more easily legitimized. If so, they did have among their number "those ordained by papal bishops" whom they could appoint to positions of authority. There was, for example, Cahera himself. Such priests, possessing valid papal orders, could call, elect, and ordain others and thus provide a continuity of ministerial order. If theories of church polity are to be classified, one might say that Luther had been urging a congregational polity as a substitute for an episcopal polity, but was willing to agree to a presbyterian polity if congregationalism seemed too extreme a solution for the problem of continuity of structure. But he went along with this expedient only for the time being, "until you grow up and fully know what is the power of the word of God." It was, then, as a temporary accommodation to their scrupulosity, not as a permanent concession to some theory of continuity, that Luther proposed the elevation to episcopal or quasi-episcopal status of Cahera and others who were in holy orders. "For it is not possible for you to accept papal ordination and those ordained by it without sin and disobedience, and therefore without risk of the destruction of souls."[6]

REJECTION OF PRIESTLY STRUCTURE

Underlying these practical recommendations was a rejection of the theory of continuity through an ordained priesthood, as well as a positive understanding of the

nature of ministerial structure and of its guarantees. Luther insisted that the mark by which the presence of the
church could be recognized was not its customs, but the
word of God. The effort to base the continuity of the
church on priestly ordination was a substitution of custom for the word, of structure for spirit. This is what
made the so-called ordination of priests an *execra-
mentum* rather than a *sacramentum* and vitiated the
claim of continuity. The Hussites had more reason to
know this than anyone else. In the bitter struggle against
them during the Hussite wars the papacy had proved itself ready to see them perish if that was necessary to
uphold the authority of ecclesiastical structures; that is,
it was willing to sacrifice both the church and its continuity for the sake of proving that its principle of continuity was the correct one. This readiness to jeopardize
continuity came in the face of the boast that it was the
one holy catholic and apostolic church, apart from which
there was no salvation. Such hypocrisy gave Luther and
his supporters the right to condemn "the church of
Rome in its insincerity and feigned authority," just as
Paul had judged Peter. In opposition, Luther insisted
that "the papal priesthood is a falsehood devised outside
the church of God and through mere effrontery brought
into the church." The very institution on which the theory of sacerdotal continuity rested had its origin outside
the church and had been foisted on the church. And so,
contrary to the charge that by elevating spirit over structure Luther and his followers had broken the continuity
of the church, it was their opponents who "have sep-
arated themselves from us and stupefied the whole
earth."[7]

Because this was the real contrast between the two theologies of structure, Luther drew a sharp opposition between his definition of the structures of the church and the papal definition, even though the latter could claim the support of a majority both past and present. He sounded the theme at the very beginning of *Concerning the Ministry:* "We are interested in the pure and true course, prescribed in holy Scripture, and are little concerned about usage or what the fathers have said or done in this matter. . . . Herein we neither ought, should, nor would be bound by human traditions, however sacred or highly regarded, but clearly exercise our reason and Christian liberty." And so the theme was repeated throughout the treatise. One should close one's eyes and open one's ears: close one's eyes to "usage, tradition, and great numbers," and open one's ears to the word of God. The word of God was a thunderbolt against which it was impossible to maintain the structure of the priesthood, in spite of "numberless fathers, innumerable councils, the custom of ages, or a majority of all the world." It was useless to argue that a majority in support of a position automatically made it right. For, as Luther declared in an aphorism that sounds proverbial, "he does not err less who errs along with many others, nor will he burn less who burns with many." Not even an angel from heaven, much less "the arguments of ancient use, the opinion of the majority, or the authority which has been recognized," could substantiate customs that had been introduced by human superstition as assurances of continuity in church structure. And in a final statement of his case he attacked those upon whom Scripture made no impression, but who were impressed "only by the use of centuries and of multitudes."[8] That was where the issue was joined, between the authority of the word and promise of God and the authority of tradition; and while Luther could argue that this made his position "the most ancient" because he was pitting apostolic antiquity against post-apostolic antiquity, he refused in principle to argue the case on the basis of the competing claims to antiquity of tradition or to continuity of legal structure.

For what was at stake was far more fundamental. It was nothing less than the gospel itself and the work of Christ as Lord and Savior. "Their madness and senselessness is such that Christ must be denied and altogether rejected so that their sacrifices and offices might survive." Nor can this be dismissed as a temporary rhetorical extravagance. In one theology, as Luther saw it, the ground of the church and of its continuity was being sought in the sacrifice of Christ, "who alone and once for all by offering himself has taken away the sins of all men and accomplished their sanctification for all eternity." In the other theology, the continuity of the church was being sought in the daily sacrifice of the body and blood of Christ at the mass "in innumerable places throughout the world," "as if his unique sacrifice were not enough, or as if he had not obtained an eternal redemption." This made the forgiveness of sins "not eternal, but repeated daily." And there the difference lay, between spirit and structure. Either continuity was to be thought of as "eternal," that is, as eternally grounded in the one, unrepeatable sacrifice of Christ, who promised that he would always be with his church and would send her his Holy Spirit; or continuity was to be thought of as "daily," that is, as passed on by the structured succession of sacrificing priests and ordaining bishops. No sophistry or compromise could soften that contrast; for "either you must attempt this way in brave faith, or else desist altogether."[9]

As the theory of the mass as a daily sacrifice was a betrayal of the eternal sacrifice of Christ, so the theory of the clergy as sacrificing priests was irreconcilable with the priesthood of Christ and with the priesthood of believers. The priesthood of believers had a positive significance for the doctrine of the ministry in *Concerning the Ministry,* to which we shall return later. But it was also part of the attack upon the priestly theory of church and ministry, which occupies the major part of the work; apparently the heading, "A priest is not identical with presbyter or minister—for one is born to be priest, one becomes a minister," belongs to the original and was not, as were so many such headings in other works of Luther, introduced by a later editor. In a point-by-point examination of the theory of priesthood and its prerogatives, Luther refuted the claim that the clergy of the church were priests. It was an unbreakable rock that "the New Testament knows of no priest who is or can be anointed externally," because a New Testament priest "is not made but is born; he is created, not ordained." And so the term "priest," properly used, could refer either to Christ as priest or to all Christians as priests, but not to the clergy. Yet Christ had become the chief priest of the New Testament without the benefit of the structure of ordination upon which the priesthood now depended, "without shaving, without anointing, and so without any of their 'character' or all the masquerade of episcopal ordination."[10] In brief, the theory of continuity of structure through the ordination of a priest by a bishop overlooked what had made priests of Christ and the apostles; and what they had lacked, it insisted upon.

Nor was it a solution of this problem when the defenders of established structure argued that "the power of the keys belongs to the church, their use, however, to the bishops." This defense against Luther's doctrine of the priesthood of believers had been attempted by some of his opponents, who sought to maintain the sacerdotal nature of the ministry, while at the same time coming to terms with the usage of the New Testament, where "priest" did indeed refer either to Christ or to believers but not to the clergy of the church. Luther's rejection of such distinctions as "fictitious" and "trifling" was, to say the least, qualified by his own application, in this same treatise, of a similar distinction to the relation between the universal priesthood of believers and the public ministry. For he wanted one or more to exercise that ministry publicly in the name of all, and he supported this on the basis of a general principle whose parallel with the argument of his opponents was more than merely verbal: "It is one thing to exercise a right publicly; another to use it in time of emergency. Publicly one may not exercise a right without consent of the whole body or of the church. In time of emergency each may use it as he deems best."[11] Certainly one difference between Luther's view here and that of his opponents lay in the prescription of how such "consent" of the church was to be obtained. But his own admission of this distinction, which was to be accented more sharply in the next two or three

years as a result of his conflict with the radical reformers, belongs to any description of his doctrine of the
ministry even in 1523.

"OUR MANNER OF APPOINTMENT, THE CHRISTIAN ONE"

In opposition to the theory of the continuity of the
church through the ordained priesthood, Luther affirmed
his own theory, "our manner of appointment, that is, the
Christian one," as he called it at the very beginning of
Concerning the Ministry. His own theological argumentation in support of his theory of church structure
must be specified with some care if the distinctness of his
position is to be identified. There is, to be sure, some reason to question whether this argumentation is basically
theological or pragmatic, for in some statements he gives
the impression that the public ministry is based on a
largely utilitarian consideration. It was on the basis of
"community of right" that he argued "that one, or as
many as the community chooses, shall be chosen or
elected who, in the name of all with these rights, shall
perform these functions publicly. Otherwise there might
be a shameful confusion among the people of God, and
a kind of Babylon in the church." The biblical support
for this arrangement, however, was not the institution
of the apostolic or ministerial office by Christ, but the
general apostolic imperative of 1 Cor. 14:40 that everything should be done "decently and in order." This
"community of right" was apparently cogent enough to
function as a general principle, just as the subordination
of the eucharist to baptism and the word, to which we

shall return in Chapter 6, was evident from the nature of the case, "even if there were no direct authority of Scripture." In the Book of Acts Stephen and Philip entered the ministry "on their own initiative and by reason of a common law." The impression that Luther's view of church structure in *Concerning the Ministry* has a decidedly pragmatic or even secular accent is reinforced when he declares that "a minister may be deposed . . . just as *any other* administrator of civil matters is treated as an equal among his brethren."[12]

Juxtaposed with this apparent pragmatism about the organized church was, as it often is, a view of the church so "high" as to seem idealistic. In the passage just quoted about deposing a minister, Luther continued: "In fact, a spiritual minister is more readily removable than any civil administrator, since if he is unfaithful he should be less tolerable than a civil officer." Advising the Utraquists rather to live without the sacraments than to go on being the victims of exploiting priests, he asserted that Christ would "not only not condemn, but surely would reward a pious and Christian abstinence from all the other sacraments [except baptism] when these would be offered by impious and sacrilegious men." Repeatedly throughout the treatise the qualifications stressed by the pastoral epistles, that the minister be "worthy," is used to warn against the ministry of impious men. On the other hand, there does not seem to be anywhere in the treatise an explicit statement of the principle upon which Luther insisted elsewhere, especially in his dealings with the Hussites, that the word and the sacraments were objectively valid even when administered by—or, for that matter, when administered to—the unworthy. There was instead the complete subordination of structure to spirit, as in the flat declaration that the sacrifices of the church can be offered "only by one who is spiritual, that is, by a Christian who has the Spirit of Christ."[13] This was combined with an attack upon the theory of objective sacramental validity, in which no effort was made to distinguish between the various possible meanings of that theory. One might conclude, then, that the continuity of the church's structure was provided exclusively by its character as a spiritual church made up of pure believers, in which the structure of the ministry was no more than a matter of convenience.

But such a conclusion would ignore the primacy of what might be called "the vertical dimension of structure" in Luther's picture of the church. If the Utraquists were afraid that they were not the church of God, they should be assured that whatever they did as believers "may be considered the work of Christ," even though they may not be shining examples of pure sainthood. The theory of continuity through the priesthood was to be rejected "not on our own authority, but on that of Christ," for the eucharistic command and promise had not been intended to institute the ordained priesthood, but had been addressed "to all who belong to him in the present and in the future." Here, in the command and promise of Christ, lay the assurance of the true continuity of structure in the church. He had promised (Matt. 18:19, 20) that where two or three were gathered together in his name, he would be in their midst, granting their requests. "If then the agreement of three or two in the name of the Lord makes all things possible, and Christ endorses as his own the things they do, how much more

may we not believe that it has happened or can happen
with his approval and guidance when we come together
in his name, pray together, and elect bishops and ministers of the word from among ourselves." The alternatives were simple and clear, as Luther formulated them
in a disjunctive syllogism: Either the church was to be
allowed to perish for lack of the word of God, or a way
had to be found to elect and install true ministers of the
word. For the continuity of structure in the church was
in that word and promise, and "it is obvious that it cannot be without the word; if it is without the word, it
ceases to be a church,"[14] regardless of the presence or absence of a "legitimately" ordained priesthood or other
proper ecclesiastical structures.

As the foundation for the church and its continuity,
the promise of Christ was not to be tampered with or
distorted. "The words of God are everywhere the same,
and we are not permitted to give them one meaning in
one place and another meaning elsewhere," as Luther
formulated the axiom of biblical interpretation. It
meant, as Luther had argued in *The Babylonian Captivity,* that the command to loose and bind sins and the
promise that they would be loosed and bound in heaven
as well (Matt. 18:18) were addressed to the entire
church and to all Christians, not merely to the ordained
priests. Those who had been called out of darkness into
light were a royal priesthood, according to 1 Peter 2:9.
"I ask, who are these who are called out of darkness into
marvelous light? Is it only the shorn and anointed
masks? Is it not all Christians?" The theory of continuity through the structure of an ordained priesthood ar-
rogated to this priesthood the rights and privileges that

belonged to all Christians. The continuity did come through a priesthood, but through the priesthood of all believers. Those who were chosen and designated as ministers "even before such election have been born and called into such a ministry through baptism."[15]

Not the sacrifices of the priesthood, but, as Luther was to insist again and again, the proclamation of the word of God assured continuity. As he had said already in *The Babylonian Captivity,* baptism, not ordination, was the sacrament of true priesthood. The head of the household could maintain the church in his family by reading the Bible and by baptism, "even if throughout life they did not dare or could not receive the eucharist." There was clearly a graduated scale of the sacraments here. Baptism was "incomparably greater" because of the word; "the eucharist is not so necessary that salvation depends on it"; and ordination, although "instituted on the authority of Scripture, and according to the example and decrees of the apostles," did not have the same explicit command as either baptism or the eucharist. This graduation of sacraments was part of a more complete stratification of means of grace, to which we shall recur in Chapter 6. Luther summarized it in a systematic statement of the true succession of ministry, a comment on the story of the Ethiopian eunuch in the eighth chapter of the Book of Acts: "Undoubtedly he taught the word of God to many, since he had the command to make known the wonderful deeds of God who called him from darkness into his marvelous light. From his word resulted the faith of many, since the word of God does not return in vain. From faith sprang a church, and the church through the word received and exercised a ministry of baptizing and teaching, and of all the other functions enumerated above. All these things a eunuch accomplished through no other right than that inherent in baptism and faith, especially in places lacking any other ministers." Therefore the Utraquists were to have no qualms about the supposed novelty of this method of selecting and installing ministers. For one thing, as we have noted, it was the rejection of "a more recent kind of plague" and the restoration of "an earlier kind of health." But even if it were an utter innovation, "when the word of God here enlightens and commands us, and the need of souls compels it, then the novelty of the thing ought not at all to affect us, but the majesty of the word [of God]." And Luther added, a little ominously: "This is a great undertaking, and the magnitude of it, rather than its novelty, impresses me."[16]

Subsequent developments proved that he had good reason to be impressed by the magnitude of the undertaking. The betrayal of his hopes for Cahera was only part of a process by which the relations between Wittenberg and the Czech Reformation came to grief. The situation in Prague, to which *Concerning the Ministry* had been addressed, proved to be altogether uncongenial to this experiment in the creation of instant structures for the church.[17] Nor were the princely or royal patrons of the new Lutheran churches in Germany and Scandinavia prepared to risk so dangerously democratic a polity. From time to time the principles of the treatise have been applied—or at least invoked—in the determination of the proper structure of the church, as when an *émigré* community in America, recapitulating in its own way the "desert island" setting of the Utraquists of Prague, reprinted *Concerning the Ministry* to prove that it was a legitimate church with a legitimate ministry.[18] To be sure, this treatise was not, even in 1523, a complete statement of Luther's theories about ministerial structure and church order; nor, for that matter, did his practice correspond with this theory or with any other single theory.[19] The fact remains, however, that *Concerning the Ministry* of 1523 is the only full-scale treatise in which Luther went on from *The Babylonian Captivity of the Church* to develop his interpretation of the priesthood and the ministry. As such, it stands as an important statement of his effort to come to terms with the problem of spirit and structure.

3

Monasticism (1523–1524)

DURING 1523, the year of his treatise *Concerning the Ministry* analyzed in Chapter 2, Luther was also attempting to cope with the structural vacuum being created by the dissolution of the religious orders. Chapter 1 has already quoted his rhetorical question in *The Babylonian Captivity* of 1520: "Will you not overturn the practice and teaching of all the churches and monasteries, by virtue of which they have flourished all these centuries?" and his forthright answer: "This is the very thing that has constrained me to write of the captivity of the church. . . . What do I care about the number and influence of those who are in this error? The truth is mightier than all of them."[1]

A year later, near the end of 1521, the beginnings of a mass exodus from the monasteries prompted him to compose a long treatise, *The Judgment of Martin Luther on Monastic Vows,* in which he set forth the theological and exegetical grounds for his attack on the threefold vow of poverty, chastity, and obedience, arguing that vows were inconsistent with Christian obedience, inimical to authentic Christian faith, hazardous to Christian liberty, alien to the demands of Christian charity, and contrary even to the precepts of sound rea-

50

son. His basic objections to monasticism in this treatise and throughout his life were theological, for he regarded it both as a false theory of Christian perfection and as a betrayal of the gospel of the free and unmerited grace of God. The strictly theological issues raised by his attack on monasticism usually get all the attention. Thus one scholar has pointed out that "at no time, not even in . . . [his earliest preserved works], did Luther maintain the traditional monastic ideal in its full scope." But when this scholar suggests that even in *The Judgment of Martin Luther on Monastic Vows* "the question of monasticism was not completely solved for Luther," he goes on to discuss further theological issues.[2]

Valid though this concentration on the theological aspects of Luther's polemic against monasticism is, it may obscure the bearing of that polemic upon the structures of the church. For the institutional structures and organized life of the church, there are few results of the Reformation more far-reaching than the sequestration of the monasteries and the abolition of the religious orders. David Knowles has called this action a "momentous decision which, far more than any of those concerned in it could have foretold, was to be of revolutionary significance not only in the religious, but also in the social and economic life of the nation."[3] Professor Knowles is speaking here specifically of the dissolution of the monasteries in England under Henry VIII, but his words apply no less to the Lutheran lands. Luther's polemic and its practical outcome not only undercut the medieval valuation of cloistered contemplation over public action, but also deprived the church of the shock troops who had been almost exclusively responsible for certain areas of her life. Three such areas were missions, welfare, and education. The virtual elimination of monasticism from the organized life of the church by the Reformation necessitated the development of new structures for all three. The significance of Luther's Reformation for the renewal of education is quite well known, but it is usually isolated from the other monastic structures of missions and welfare—and with good reason, since Luther's achievements in these two areas of ministry are considerably less impressive than is his role in the development of new structures for Christian education. For an understanding of Luther's "character in crisis" as shown in his treatment of church structures, his "philosophy of education" is less useful than a study of the implications of the abolition of the religious orders.

MISSIONS

Together with most of the other Christians of Europe, Luther owed his Christian inheritance to the work of the medieval monks. He acknowledged, in a treatise to be analyzed in the next chapter, that "everything that is Christian and good is to be found [under the papacy] and has come to us from this source." He knew, too, that none of the original apostles had come to the Germanic tribes, and he joked that though Christ had had only twelve apostles, there were eighteen buried in Germany. In 1522 he noted that "Germany was converted about 800 years after the apostles," and added that "recently many islands and lands have been discovered, to which this grace [of God] has not appeared for these 1500 years." Although Luther was thus aware, at least to some extent, of the historical circumstances surrounding the Christianization of Europe, he does not refer to them very often. Among those circumstances, one of the most important was, in the words of Kenneth Scott Latourette, that for much of Christian history "the large majority of the missionaries were monks. But for monks, indeed, it is hard to see how in most regions the expansion of Christianity could have been carried on. But for them it would have proceeded much more slowly and would have remained more superficial." This judgment becomes all the more significant when it is placed alongside another statement by the same historian. Contrasting the spectacular accomplishments of Roman Catholicism in the conversion of the New World with the late start of Protestantism, Professor Latourette suggests, among other reasons, that "Protestantism lacked the monks who for more than a thousand years had been the chief agents for propagating the faith. Even when they were interested in giving the gospel to non-Christians, Protestants did not have ready-to-hand machinery for spreading it among non-Christians."[4]

Latourette's words, "even when they were interested in giving the gospel to non-Christians," should be noted. For the only non-Christians in whose evangelization Luther seems to have had very much interest were Jews and Muslims. In the early years of the Reformation Luther believed that the evangelization of the Jews had been so unsuccessful because the gospel had been suppressed under the papacy. "But now that the golden light of the gospel is rising and radiating a bright beam, there is the hope that many from among the Jews will be converted in a more sincere and honest way [than they had been under the papacy] and thus let themselves be moved from the world to Christ." Luther's hopes about the conversion of the Jews were disappointed, and his disappointment expressed itself during his later years in a treatise against the Jews about which even so sympathetic a biographer as Roland H. Bainton has said: "One could wish that Luther had died before ever this tract was written."[5] Thus his interest in the Christianization of the Jews never developed an appropriate structure; it did not get beyond the stage of hope, and even that did not last long. Lacking such a structure, or what Professor Latourette calls "ready-to-hand machinery for spreading [the gospel] among non-Christians," the Reformation's mission to the Jews fell stillborn.

The closest Luther ever came to proposing a structure for the missionary task was a suggestion that arose in the course of his writing about the menace of the Turks. Most of that writing was devoted to a careful effort to disengage himself from any notion of a crusade or holy war in which the secular government would be fighting to defend the cause of the gospel. It was indeed the duty of the emperor to fight, but not in the name of the Christian faith. Turning his attention to the plight of those Christians who had been captured and enslaved by the Turks and who must now try to practice their faith in a Muslim land, Luther urged them to be faithful slaves of their Turkish masters. Struck by the parallel between their situation and that of the early Christians in the Roman empire, he counseled:

"All you will ever accomplish with resistance and impatience is to irritate your master, whose slave you have become, and thus make him more cruel. In addition, you will slander the doctrine and the name of Christ, as though Christians were the sort of wicked, unfaithful, and false people who do not serve but run away, who want to enrich themselves as scoundrels and thieves. In this way [your master] will become even more confirmed and obdurate in his belief. On the other hand, if you serve him faithfully and diligently, you will adorn and enhance the gospel and the name of Christ, so that your master and perhaps some others, regardless of how wicked they might be, will have to say: 'Well, well! Those Christians are certainly a faithful, obedient, pious, humble, and diligent people!' Thus you would also overthrow the faith of the Turks and perhaps convert many, if they were to see that the Christians are so superior to the Turks in humility, patience, diligence, faithfulness, and similar virtues. This is what St. Paul means when he says in the third chapter of Titus [Titus 2:10.]: 'Slaves should adorn or enhance the doctrine of our Lord in everything.' "[6]

This was undeniably a moving expression of the strategy to be followed by an individual Christian who had been taken prisoner of war by Muslims and who needed encouragement in the path of Christian duty. But it was considerably less than a proposal to replace the structure of the missionary orders, whose monastic rules Luther had repudiated, with some other structure that would carry on the missionary imperative. Luther's failure to propose such a structure was not based on indifference to the missionary imperative contained in the gospel.[7] Repeatedly he gave voice to that imperative as an inescapable corollary of Christian faith. Christians had to address the gospel to others not only (perhaps not even primarily) because the others were outside the church, but because of the dynamic of the gospel itself; and the gospel they addressed to "the world" was the same as that addressed to "the church."

From the words quoted earlier and from several other statements like them it is evident that Luther knew about the islands of the sea which had just been discovered and were still being discovered, where there would be men "to whom no one has preached" the gospel. About the imperative to preach it to them, there was no ambiguity; about the method and the structure for preaching it, there seems to have been little more than improvisation. The only non-Christians of whom he was at all directly aware were not pagans, but adherents of one or another "book monotheism." Yet even in order to convert an Islam that was battering at the gates of Christian Europe and a Judaism that dwelt within those gates, he could not devise a structure that could serve as an evangelical substitute for the monks. A century and a half were to pass before his followers could begin to produce such a structure.

WELFARE

In proposing structures to substitute for the institutions of monasticism in the field of welfare, Luther was somewhat more concrete—concrete enough, in any event, to devote a special treatise, albeit a brief one, to such structures. He was even more concrete in his criticism of the existing monastic structures for dealing with the problems of human need. The most conspicuous among these was begging, or, to use the more theological term, mendicancy. By Luther's time this practice certainly deserved the honorific "structure," for it had become an administrative institution in its own right. The medieval church had been caught up in a series of controversies over the ideal of poverty demanded by the New Testament as a mark of the true disciples of Christ.[9] One outcome of those controversies was the emergence and stabilization of the mendicant orders as an institutional embodiment of that ideal, though not without bitter resistance both from the older religious orders and from the diocesan clergy.

Luther rejected this entire development as a distortion of what had been intended by the ideal of property expressed in the first of the Beatitudes, "Blessed are the poor in spirit." Repeatedly throughout his writings Luther attacked the notion that this poverty in spirit was attainable only in the so-called "angelic life" of the monastic orders. The Sermon on the Mount was speaking not about structures of poverty, but about a poverty in spirit, "so that nothing is accomplished when someone is physically poor and has no money or goods. . . . This does not mean, therefore, that one must be poor in the sense of having nothing at all of his own. . . . There is many a beggar getting bread at our door more arrogant and wicked than any rich man." "From this have come the pope's monks, who on the basis of this chapter have laid claim to a more perfect station in life than other Christians." But the summons to discipleship in the Beatitudes was not a series of "evangelical counsels," intended only for the spiritual athletes in the

cloisters. It was addressed to all, and Christ had threatened "that no one will enter heaven who abolishes even
one of the least of these commandments, and he explicitly calls them 'commandments.' " Thus the ideal of
poverty was not to be realized within the structures of
the monastic orders, for it was a matter of the spirit.[10]
This new portrait of the ordinary Christian rather than
the full-time ascetic as the true beggar before God represented a radical break with the traditional ethics of
Western Christianity.

It also implied an attack on the institution of mendicancy. "One of the greatest necessities," wrote Luther
to the Christian nobility, "is the abolition of all begging
throughout Christendom." Particularly reprehensible in
his eyes was the itinerancy of the mendicant orders, each
of which, on its rounds, visited the same town six or
seven times a year. With five or six mendicant orders,
this amounted to almost a weekly invasion of every town
by begging monks. Added to the regular rounds of other
beggars, including the "ambassador beggars," this
meant, in Luther's words, that "up to sixty times a year
a town is laid under tribute!" The practice of begging,
moreover, was filled with "skulduggery and deceit," and
it encouraged "vagabonds and evil rogues" to take un-
fair advantage of the Christian charity of the common
people. The history of legislation, both civil and ecclesiastical, aimed at cutting down the excesses of profes-
sional mendicancy shows that Luther was touching here
on an aspect of monasticism that was subject to constant
and almost inevitable abuse. What he proposed was another way of coping with "poverty," both with poverty
as an evangelical ideal and with poverty as a social and

economic reality. As an evangelical ideal, poverty was
not to be identified with the ascetic renunciation of property by the full-time religious; as a social and economic
reality, it was indeed the proper object of Christian
charity, but some way had to be found to protect that
charity from being exploited. The two definitions of poverty were, of course, closely tied together in practice;
for, as Professor Hussey has said of Byzantine Christianity, "to care for the poor was a Christian duty which
fell on all, and it was one of the special obligations of
the monastic world."[11]

In 1521, addressing the problem of how to cope with
poverty now that the monastic institutions of mercy were
disappearing, Luther endorsed the widespread laws requiring that every city take the responsibility to provide
for its own poor and prohibiting itinerant mendicancy by
monks and other beggars. The city should have an over-
seer or warden who would know the resident poor and
inform the city council of their needs. He added: "Or
some other better arrangement might be made." The
opportunity to put forth practical proposals for some
other better arrangement arose two years later. The village of Leisnig in Electoral Saxony had for some time
been negotiating with Luther and inviting him for a
visit, as he reported in a letter dated September 25,
1522. Soon thereafter, probably in January, 1523, Luther received a copy of the ordinance they were proposing for a common chest. He wrote to them expressing
his approval as well as his hope "that it will redound
both to the glory of God and as a good example of
Christian faith and love to many people. I wish and
pray that this intention and plan of yours will be blessed,

strengthened, and perfected by God through the richness of his grace." To that end Luther promised to publish the ordinance together with his preface, and apparently did so soon thereafter.[12] The preface is a trenchant little essay on the constituent elements of a truly evangelical ordinance to provide financial support for the ministry of the church to those in need.

In commending the members of the parish at Leisnig for their zeal, which, like that of the Corinthians (cf. 2 Cor. 9:2), had stirred up others to follow their example, Luther expressed his hope that this would have as its result "a great decline in the existing foundations, monastic houses, chapels, and those horrible dregs which have until now battened on the wealth of the whole world under the pretense of serving God." He complained that by this time his movement was being cited as the culprit in one social calamity after another. He fully expected that he would "have to take the blame whenever monasteries and foundations are vacated, when the number of monks and nuns decreases, and whenever anything else happens to diminish and damage the 'spiritual' estate." Here he was reacting to the constant charge that the elevation of spirit over structure in his reformatory program was undercutting such agencies as the mendicant orders, by which various Christian ministries, including welfare, had been carried on. As we have seen from *The Babylonian Captivity,* Luther recognized these implications and did not shrink from them. Here he reinforced that recognition, putting it in the form of a "sincere warning" and a "kind request" to his readers. A reader was entitled to follow through on Luther's proposals only if he "realizes and thoroughly understands from the gospel that the monastic and 'spiritual' estates, as they have been for the past four hundred years, serve no useful purpose and are nothing but harmful error and deception."[13] There was, then, to be a clean break with the monastic ideal, both among the common Christians and, if possible, among the inmates of the monasteries themselves.

As in the case of other structures discussed in this book, however, so especially in the case of the monasteries, Luther's Reformation could not simply decree a clean break with medieval Christendom without some determination about how to dispose of existing institutions. Something had to be done about the inmates of the monasteries and about the monastic properties. Although it would have been best if monastic institutions had not arisen in the first place, "now that they are here, the best thing is to let them dwindle away, or, where it can properly be done, to assist them to disappear altogether." This implied, above all, that no monastic vow was to be regarded as binding for life, and that therefore monks were to be allowed, "if they so desire, to leave of their own free will, as the gospel permits." There would, understandably, be some monks "who because of their age, their bellies, or their consciences elect to remain in the monastery." They were not to be forced to leave, but were to be assured of lifelong support. But this seems to have applied only to those who had already made their monastic profession before the Reformation took over, rather than to any who, even after the Reformation had begun, might still be minded to assume the cowl. There was evangelical freedom to leave the monastery or to remain in the monastery, but not to enter the monastery and take the vows. For it was the responsibility of the secular government to work out arrangements "with the monasteries under its jurisdiction to admit no further applicants and, if there are too many inmates, to send the excess elsewhere and let the remainder die out."[14]

The introduction of the civil authorities as the proper agency for presiding over the dissolution of the monastic institutions was part of the fateful process by which, in many areas of church life, Luther's Reformation repudiated the structures of church administration in the name of the freedom of the spirit, only to end up exchanging these structures for the structures of political administration. The responsibility of the civil authorities extended not only to the disposition of the previous inmates of the monasteries, but also to the expropriation of the holdings of the monasteries, or, more precisely, to the two problems together. Luther recommended that the civil authorities "take over the property of such monasteries, and from it make provision for those inmates who choose to remain there, until they die." They were to be provided for more generously than they had been under the monastic establishments, to make it clear "that this is not a case of greed opposing clerical possession, but of Christian faith opposing monasticism."[15] Once the last of the inmates of a monastery had died out, of course, any such arrangement would be terminated, so that the authorities would have to support the remaining monks only for a time and then would have the monastic property for themselves, free and clear.

Despite the insistence that this was not a case of greed opposing clerical possessions but of Christian faith opposing monasticism, there was clearly room for greed to cloak itself in reformatory zeal. "We have to expect," Luther acknowledged, "that greed will creep in here and there." The widespread disaffection with the monastic and "spiritual" estates would have brought on some sort of reaction in any case, quite apart from the Reformation; but Luther foresaw that his campaign against monastic institutions would help to set off a wholesale secularization of their holdings, and he was determined "to the extent of my ability and duty to forestall such a catastrophe while there is still time." He counseled great care "lest there be a mad scramble for the assets of such vacated foundations, and everyone makes off with whatever he can lay his hands on." He recommended that heirs who had been deprived of their inheritance because an ancestor had willed his property to a monastic establishment have the right to reclaim it; but he admitted the validity of the objection that "on that basis the common chest will receive precious little, for everyone will claim the whole amount and say that his needs are great." Realistically Luther also admitted that he did not expect his counsel to be accepted by the "greedy bellies" who were about to "grab these ecclesiastical possessions and claim as an excuse that I was the one who put them up to it."[16] By speaking out as he did, Luther wanted to exonerate himself beforehand and to assign the blame for the catastrophe elsewhere. The monasteries must go in any event; the question was what would happen to their assets.

One possibility was that "mendicant houses located in cities might be converted into good schools for boys and girls, as they were before." As we shall note later in this chapter, Luther made more of this idea in some of his proposals for the reform of education. But he recognized that not all the cloisters had been intended as schools, and that it would neither be practical to convert all of them into schools nor satisfactory to neglect the other needs which they had been serving. He recommended three ways to use the assets of the confiscated properties. As has already been noted, he urged that those who wanted to remain in the monasteries have security for life. Secondly, he recognized that many of those who had been in the religious life would have to be retrained before going back into the world, and he proposed that they be compensated for the years they had spent behind monastery walls. "The third way is the best, however, to devote all the remaining property to the common fund of a common chest, out of which gifts and loans could be made in Christian love to all the needy in the land." This is what the Christian citizens of Leisnig had done in the ordinance for which Luther was composing this preface. If this ordinance and his suggestions were put into practice, there would be "a well-filled common chest for every need," and various economic evils, including begging, would be eliminated. Yet he was "setting down this advice only in accordance with Christian love, and for Christians only," and he wanted matters "to be determined by Christian love and not by strict human justice."[17] He would not be so presumptuous as to legislate for others about structures for the ministry of welfare.

Subsequent developments suggest that he was, if anything, not presumptuous enough. The Leisnig experiment itself foundered badly. Luther's correspondence documents how the situation deteriorated. On August 11, 1523, he wrote to the Elector Frederick to report on a visit to Leisnig, where he had discovered that "the property which has previously been 'spiritual' and which many have used for wicked foundations and abuses, has not yet been handed over." He warned Frederick that further delay would confirm the suspicions of those who charged that the cause of the Reformation would bring with it a breakdown of the church's ministry, and he urged that these slanders be stopped by speedy action. On August 19 of the same year he wrote to Frederick again, prodding him to act. "For even though some of [the citizens of Leisnig] may have a false opinion, the ordinance is still Christian; and regardless of who may be pious or wicked, I am only concerned that idolatry may be reinstated and that the gospel may fall and be blasphemed, because there is no salary with which to maintain preachers, pastors, and other offices, and the poor must also suffer want." More than a year later, on November 24, 1524, Luther complained to Spalatin regarding the elector's continued delay in doing something about Leisnig: "Why is the prince delaying? But we are inclined to believe that because of this situation good men who are forsaken this way will resign from their parishes. Or will they not rather be driven back into the monasteries? This exceedingly unfortunate case vexes me very much; for as it was the first, it also ought to have been the best."[18]

Nor was the fiasco at Leisnig an isolated instance, as Luther's correspondence and other writings show. On January 22, 1525, two months after the letter just quoted, Luther wrote to John Lang: "Although we are poor here ourselves, we are overwhelmed daily [with poor people]. Our church is burdened with poor strangers, while we are unable even to do right by our own poor. Erfurt, meanwhile, that great and horrible city, which is situated in a lush place and is richer and more fertile than we, is able to support more of them. If only somehow the power of the word would take hold!" On September 16, 1527, Luther wrote to the Elector John of Saxony, requesting that the Franciscan cloister in Wittenberg be converted into a poorhouse, given as "as inn and dwelling to our Lord Jesus Christ for his poor members, since he has said [Matt. 25:40]: 'As you did it to one of the least of these my brethren, you did it to me.' " The following year Luther wrote a foreword to a new edition of the *Book of Vagabonds,* once more complaining that he was being overwhelmed by paupers and beggars and once more recommending the procedure he had urged in the preface to the Leisnig ordinance five years earlier: "Let every city and village know and be acquainted with its own poor, as listed in a catalogue, to help them, and not put up with foreign or alien beggars without a letter of reference or other attestation. For all sorts of rascality goes on in this matter, as this book shows. But if every city kept track of its poor this way, that rascality would soon be avoided and abolished." And in 1533, ten years after the Leisnig incident, Luther wrote another foreword on the subject, this time to a book by Caspar Adler, *A Sermon on Almsgiving.*[19] Here he expressed his disgust at the greed that posed as evangelical Christianity, his disappointment at what was happening to the level of support in the churches, and his despair over the possibility of any change in the broad masses.

In the field of welfare, Luther's Reformation had proceeded on the expectation that Christian love, animated by the Spirit, could be relied upon to carry out the ministry to the needy, and that the monastic structures inherited from the Middle Ages were worse than useless. Luther summarized the pathos both of that expectation and of its frustration less than a year after his Leisnig preface when he said, in a sermon on the office of deacon in the apostolic church: "It would be good, if there were people available for it, if such a city as this were to be divided into four or five sectors. To each one there would be assigned a preacher and a deacon, who would distribute goods, care for the sick, and see who is suffering need. But we do not have the personnel for this; therefore I do not think we can put it into effect until God makes Christians."[20]

EDUCATION

Of all the structures of medieval life whose existence was threatened by the abolition of the religious orders, education was by far the most prominent in Luther's mind.[21] He himself was well aware of the importance of monasticism for education. If anything, he exaggerated it, for he supposed that this had been a primary responsibility of the orders since their founding. In *The Judgment of Martin Luther on Monastic Vows,* discussing voluntary vows as "an institution of the primitive church," he declared: "The first Christian schools came from this practice. . . . Colleges and monasteries eventually developed from these early beginnings." But now, he complained, these "free Christian schools have been made into servile Jewish monasteries, which are actually nothing but synagogues of ungodliness." He went on to propose that these institutions be restored to what he regarded as their primitive purpose. "Monasteries would then have the character God intended for them to have and nothing else. They would simply be Christian schools for youth, designed to establish ardent young people in the faith by means of a godly upbringing."[22] If vows could be made voluntary and if the education of the young could be recovered as the chief task of the monastic establishments, Luther foresaw a possible role for them even in the reformed ecclesiastical structure for which he was working.

In education as in welfare, however, events moved faster than Luther had anticipated, so that a year or so after the preface to the common chest at Leisnig he had to turn his attention also to education, in the first and most important of his so-called "pedagogical writings," *To the Councilmen of All Cities in Germany that They Establish and Maintain Christian Schools,* written early in 1524. Here, he called education the reason why "the monasteries and foundations originated," adding that "they have since been perverted to a different and damnable use." He was speaking from his own experience as a monk when he described the libraries established by "the monasteries and foundations of old," but he was critical of them because "they neglected to acquire books and good libraries at that time, when the books and men for it were available." Instead, the monks had "devoured all our goods and filled every monastery, indeed every nook and cranny, with the filth and dung of their foul and poisonous books, until it is appalling to think of it." In this connection he also took note of the financial support which the religious orders and other institutions of the medieval church had received, a support which, he argued, could now better be diverted to the cause of Christian education. The monastic schools were "nothing but devourers and destroyers of children," because they had failed to carry out their educational tasks. He attacked "those devil's masks, the monks, and those phantoms which are the universities, which we endowed with vast properties."[23] Specifically, Luther's attack on monastic education was directed not only at the library, as we have already noted, but especially at the faculty and at the curriculum.

For the faculty of the typical monastery school Luther expressed bitter contempt. "The tonsured crowd," he said, "are unfit to teach or to rule, for all they know is to care for their bellies, which is indeed all they have been taught." He described them as "teachers and masters who knew nothing themselves, and were incapable of teaching anything good or worthwhile. In fact, they did not even know how to study or teach." He blamed the incompetence of the faculties on the vicious circle of monks teaching other monks on the basis of textbooks written by still other monks, with nothing but monastic books available to either students or teachers. His comments here in *To the Councilmen of Germany* should be supplemented by the anecdotal material that appears in his *Table Talk* and elsewhere, in which he recounted some of the choice instances of the ignorance of the

monks. He seems to have taken a special delight in expos-
ing their innocence of classical languages and literature.
His oft-repeated attack on the "divisions and sects"
among the monastic orders, who wanted nothing to do
with monks under a different rule, also contained the
implication that such isolation only fostered ignorance
by depriving them of enlightenment from other sources.[24]
If there was to be educational reform, there had to be a
new breed of teacher.

There also had to be a drastic revision of the curriculum. Here perhaps more than anywhere else in his
thought, Luther joined himself to the cause of the humanists in the call for thoroughgoing reform. Praising
these adherents of the new learning as "the finest and
most learned group of men, adorned with languages and
all the arts," Luther asked: "What have men been
learning till now in the universities and monasteries except to become asses, blockheads, and numbskulls?" So
disgusted was he with the traditional curriculum and with
its results that he was willing to conclude: "If universities and monasteries were to continue as they have been
in the past, and there were no other place available
where youth could study and live, then I could wish that
no boy would ever study at all, but just remain dumb."
The revival of learning by the humanists was beginning
to provide men who could teach the youth properly; it
was also setting forth proposals for changes in the subject matter of education at all levels. This was a time in
which God had "graciously bestowed upon us an abun-
dance of arts, scholars, and books," a real "year of
jubilee" for German culture.[25] The old-fashioned curriculum of the monastic schools simply was not adequate

to the new needs and new opportunities of the day.

Luther's critique of the old-fashioned monastic curriculum and his proposals for curricular reform concentrated on the study of the biblical and classical languages. He charged the monks with having been hostile to the study of the languages; "Indeed, they have always raged against languages and are even now raging." Their hostility to the languages was theological in its basis and demonic in its origin. "We do not see many instances," he said, "where the devil has allowed [the languages] to flourish by means of the universities and monasteries." The devil had stirred up the monks against the languages, for he knew "that if the languages were revived a hole would be knocked in his kingdom which he could not easily stop up again." To oppose this demonic plot, it was vital that the study of the biblical and classical languages be established and preserved. But "if through our neglect we let the languages go (which God forbid!), we shall not only lose the gospel, but the time will come when we shall be unable to speak or write a correct Latin or German." In support of this educational principle, Luther cited "the deplorable and dreadful example of the universities and monasteries, in which men have not only unlearned the gospel, but have in addition so corrupted the Latin and German languages that the miserable folk have been fairly turned into beasts, unable to speak or write a correct German or Latin, and have well-nigh lost their natural reason to boot."[26] Thus the cultural level of the monastic schools and their religious level were, in Luther's judgment, closely related.

Luther's attack on the monastic schools had, by the

time of the composition of *To the Councilmen of Germany,* helped to precipitate a crisis in education similar to that which we have noted in missions and in welfare. Luther himself admitted that "schools are everywhere being left to go to wrack and ruin. The universities are growing weak, and monasteries are declining." People had begun to recognize "how un-Christian these institutions are," and their support for the monasteries and monastic schools had declined accordingly. Unfortunately, this decline in support was not being matched by a corresponding rise in support for Protestant institutions. Now that the average citizen was rid of the "pillage and compulsory giving" associated with the support of the monastic establishments, he should "contribute a part of that amount toward schools for the training of the poor children." The devil was responsible "when men gave their money for monasteries and masses, pouring it out in a veritable stream," but he objected when they supported truly Christian education. There was great danger, then, that Germany would "let our schools go by the board and fail to replace them with others that are Christian."[27] The crisis was urgent, for the old structures were dying and the new structures had not yet been born.

Aggravating the crisis was a by-product of the spirit of the Reformation, a growing anti-intellectualism. In part, this disparagement of learning was the product of the materialism of the age, which looked upon education in a purely utilitarian way and therefore could not understand the value of foreign languages even though it was eager for foreign wares. But quite unintentionally Luther had helped to abet this anti-intellectualism by his violent attacks on the monastic schools and universities, on their textbooks and teachers. In education as in liturgy, Luther's colleague, Carlstadt, sought to carry out all the way what Luther had announced in theory. By the time of *To the Councilmen of Germany* Carlstadt had launched his campaign against formal education, repudiating his own academic degrees on the basis of Matt. 23:10 and dissuading students from continuing at the university. Certain groups among the Hussites, too, had been minimizing the importance of the biblical languages. "We should not be led astray because some boast of the Spirit," warned Luther, the champion of Spirit over structure. "Dear friend, say what you will about the Spirit, I too have been in the Spirit and have seen the Spirit. . . . I know full well that while it is the Spirit alone who accomplishes everything, I would surely have never flushed a covey if the languages had not helped me."[28] Spirit there had to be, yes, but there also had to be that structure of learning which only formal schooling could provide.

It was to meet this crisis created by the dissolution of the monasteries and of the monastic schools that Luther turned to the councilmen of Germany. With the departure of the monks, the councilmen were the only proper authorities to step in. For one of the most far-reaching implications of Luther's thought for education was a new concentration on training for public service. Monastic education had despised public service as something beneath the dignity of the perfect Christian. The monks had "shown no concern whatever for the temporal government, and have designed their schools so exclusively for the 'spiritual' estate that it has become almost a disgrace for an educated man to marry." Nevertheless, "temporal government has to continue." And if it was to continue, there had to be educational structures whose task it was to train men for service in the government. In a sense, government needed "good schools and educated persons even more than the spiritual realm." This was evident even from the conclusions of reason, as well as from the educational achievements of ancient, pagan Rome. On the basis of his reading of Cicero, Quintilian, and other Latin writers, Luther was deeply impressed by the quality of man produced in Roman schools. It was a man who knew the languages, studied the liberal arts, and served the common weal. "Their system produced intelligent, wise, and competent men, so skilled in every art and rich in experience that if all the bishops, priests, and monks in the whole of Germany today were rolled into one, you would not have the equal of a single Roman soldier."[29]

Because it was a responsibility of the schools to train such men for public service, the councilmen had both the right and the duty to concern themselves with developing the structures of education. Luther devoted a long section of *To the Councilmen of Germany* to an exposition, based both on the Old Testament and on the New, of the duty of parents to provide for the education of the young. To the objection that "all that is spoken to the parents; what business is it of councilmen and the authorities?" Luther replied that some parents lacked the goodness and decency to do their duty, that most parents lacked the ability, and that almost all parents lacked the time and opportunity. "Is it for this reason to be left undone, and the children neglected? How will the authorities and council then justify their position, that such matters are not their responsibility?" Similarly, it could be argued that if the common man was "incapable of it, unwilling, and ignorant of what to do, princes and lords ought to be doing it." True, the princes did have a responsibility for the education of their subjects; but Luther, knowing the way of life at the German courts, feared that most of them were so "burdened with high and important functions in cellar, kitchen, and bedroom" that they could not be bothered with the schools. And so it was up to the councilmen, who, for that matter, had "a better authority and occasion to do it than princes and lords." Luther admonished them: "Therefore, dear sirs, take this task to heart which God so earnestly requires of you, which your office imposes upon you, which is so necessary for our youth, and which neither the spiritual realm nor the secular realm can do without."[30]

Like the other structures we are examining in this volume, this system of education was projected on the tacit assumption that the councilmen of Germany would be equally concerned with the welfare of the spiritual and the secular realm. Even in the short-range perspective of the remaining two decades of Luther's life, this assumption proved to be false. Luther's faith that the Spirit could dispense with the monastic structures was accompanied by the hope that the Spirit would, by creating true Christians, call forth the establishment of new and more authentic structures. The faith was sound, the hope was illusory. He had spoken more prophetically than he recognized when he said, in the words quoted earlier: "But we do not have the personnel for this;

therefore I do not think we can put it into effect until God makes Christians." No such structure for missions was erected; the structures for welfare were a series of unworkable makeshifts; and even the educational structures came into the hands of princes who proved to be even less responsive to the gospel than the religious orders had been. Although this outcome of his campaign did not by any means prompt Luther to soften his attack on monasticism, it did play its role in his growing recognition during the later 1520's and afterward that it was easier to denounce corruption in existing structures than it was to devise structures free of corruption. Beneath that recognition was the even more profound conviction that the continuity of Christian faith and life—and therefore even the continuity of Christian institutions— was worth preserving. In Luther's defense of infant baptism, to which we turn now in Chapter 4, that continuity was to be a decisive factor.

4

The Problem of Infant Baptism (1527–1528)

A CENTRAL FACTOR in Luther's polemic against the clerical structures of the institutional church, as summarized in Chapters 2 and 3, was his rejection, as a priest, of the "indelible character" of his ordination and his repudiation, as a monk, of the lifelong obligation of his threefold vow. But another "indelible character" in the official theory about church structures was that conferred in baptism; another vow whose lifelong validity was basic to the Christian life was likewise that professed in baptism. If anything, Luther's elevation of spirit over structure and his stress on faith made it even more essential that the baptismal vow be taken freely and consciously. Similarly, his classification of the sacraments, outlined in Chapter 2, elevated baptism to a decisive place, but interpreted it in such a way that any quasi-magical view of its efficacy seemed to be illegitimate. It was reasonable in the light of this for many of his contemporaries to conclude that Luther's position, consistently carried out, would undercut the traditional doctrine and practice of the church regarding infant baptism.

Despite his many references to the Anabaptists throughout the last two decades of his life, Luther knew very little about the group who drew such a radical conclusion from his thought. It seems clear that he probably never saw a genuine Anabaptist face-to-face. Moreover, he persisted in his identification of the Anabaptists with other opponents who had no direct connection with them, even when he had the opportunity to become more precisely informed about the differences. While several of his colleagues did gather firsthand data about Anabaptism, Luther seems to have been content with the rumors he got from others and the suspicions he had within himself, and on this basis he formed his judgments. But it is important to keep the question of Luther's knowledge of Anabaptism distinct from the question of his defense of infant baptism. The former could have been changed by more accurate reportage, but the latter could not have been changed by anything less drastic than a fundamental theological reorientation. Luther's defense of infant baptism was not, as has been supposed, part of a "doctrine of the sacraments [in which] Luther abandoned his position as a reformer, and was guided by views that brought confusion into his own system of faith"; nor is it accurate to contend that "if the fundamental evangelical and Lutheran principle is valid . . . then infant baptism is in itself no sacrament, but an *ecclesiastical* observance."[1] On the contrary, Luther's defense of infant baptism, like his defense of the real presence in the eucharist, was inseparable from "the fundamental evangelical and Lutheran principle."

That principle, however, was not simply "that grace

and faith are inseparably interrelated," but a more subtle and complex principle, namely, that faith and the word were inseparably interrelated, also in the sacraments, and moreover, that also in the sacraments "faith builds and is founded on the word of God rather than God's word on faith." This was the most fundamental issue in the controversy over infant baptism, as Luther interpreted it. How Luther interpreted the controversy is, however, more difficult to determine in detail than one might expect, for in spite of many comments on the Anabaptists throughout his writings and lectures he devoted only one full-length treatise to the defense of infant baptism, the essay *Concerning Rebaptism. A Letter of Martin Luther to Two Pastors,* written in December 1527 and January 1528 in response to the request of two otherwise unidentified pastors for arguments against the Anabaptist position.[2] Although the issue was to recur in later works of Luther, where he made use of some of the same arguments, the treatise of 1528 deserves to be studied closely, as a special aspect of Luther's thought on spirit and structure.

THE ARGUMENT FROM THE FAITH OF INFANTS

In *Concerning Rebaptism* Luther took up the charge of the Anabaptists that faith was prerequisite to baptism and that since children could not believe, they were not to be baptized. He claimed to have read that they were citing the words of Mark 16:16, "He who believes and is baptized will be saved," as proof of this charge. But if they wanted to argue from this passage of Scripture that faith was prerequisite to baptism, they also had to produce proof from Scripture that children were incapable of faith. For his part, Luther found proof in Scripture, both in the Old Testament and in the New, "that children may and can believe, even though they have neither speech nor reason." He was careful to point out that this proof did not yet establish that children did in fact have faith, only that they might and could. This presentation of biblical evidence shows how "commentary and controversy" interacted in Luther's use of Scripture. It is also an index to his affinities with the exegetical, dogmatic, and legal tradition of the Middle Ages. For the appropriate arguments from Augustine in defense of the thesis that children could believe had been assembled in the *Corpus of the Canon Law*. On the basis of these arguments, the biblical evidence had been exploited with increasing care and profundity by early scholasticism and had been carried as far as it could be, until the speculative doctrine of the infusion of faith provided theologians with a method for gathering additional proof texts.[3] Despite his hostility both to the canon law and to speculation, Luther seems in fact to have been drawing on this material here in *Concerning Rebaptism*.

The first passage Luther cited was Ps. 106:38: "They poured out innocent blood." If the blood of children sacrificed to idols was innocent, the children must have had faith. The second proof was taken from the story of Herod's murder of the children of Bethlehem. They, too, were "innocent," Luther argued. To be sure, the text of the gospel does not say that they were, but they had acquired the title *Innocentes* in the liturgical usage of the church at Rome, being called simply *Infantes* in other orders and calendars. And from this designation, embellished by medieval piety, Luther maintained that they were "holy and were saved" even though they had neither speech nor reason. The third passage was Matt. 19:14: "Let the children come to me . . . for to such belongs the kingdom of heaven." Tertullian's denial of the appropriateness of these words to infant baptism suggests that as early as the second century they were already being applied that way. Luther, following the established usage of pre-Reformation Wittenberg, had incorporated them in his *Order of Baptism* of 1523 and of 1526. The fourth passage was the account of the visitation, in which John the Baptist "in the womb leaped for joy" (Luke 1:44). The observance of the visitation had finally received conciliar sanction a century before, and Luther's interpretation of the words of the gospel reflected the traditional observance.[4]

The relation between the faith of infants and the baptism of infants was a matter of continuing concern to Luther both before and after *Concerning Rebaptism*. It seems clear that Luther did not place less emphasis on infant faith during 1528 and 1529 than he had earlier. His constant reference to his earlier statements on the matter proves that he never repudiated his earlier affirmations that children received the gift of faith through baptism. On the other hand, it is evident even from the argumentation here in *Concerning Rebaptism* that Luther, in contradistinction to at least some parts of the dogmatic tradition, was not willing to let the defense of infant baptism depend so utterly on the theory of infant faith that the two teachings would stand or fall together. Martin Luther may well have been the one theologian in the history of the church who, more than any other, elevated faith to the status of a normative principle in Christian theology; he himself seems sometimes to have seen his historic role this way. But when it came to the relation between faith and the means of grace, or at any rate to the relation between faith and infant baptism, he did not assign the decisive importance to faith, but gave it to the structured mediation of divine grace in baptism. And so, immediately after his recitation of the traditional exegetical proofs for infant faith, he declared: "Anyone who wants to use the faith of the person to be baptized as the basis for baptism may never again baptize any one; for even if you were to baptize the same man a hundred times in one day, you would not know a single one of those times whether he believes." Theologian of faith though he quite self-consciously was, Luther would not make infant faith the determinative issue in his defense of infant baptism— even though it is clear that Luther had no qualms about ascribing faith to infants and that he would even go so far as to say, as he did here, that infant baptism was surer than adult baptism, for the very reason that made it so problematical to the Anabaptists, the absence of personal, subjective assent.[5]

The defense of infant baptism, then, could not be based solely on the assertion that infants could have faith, whether through the infusion of faith in baptism itself or through the faith of their parents or through the faith of mother church. This made it necessary to provide other grounds for the practice that would, if not indeed supplant, at least supplement the historic argument from the faith of infants. And though Luther was

a theologian of faith, he was also, perhaps even more, a
theologian of the structured means of divine grace. As a
theologian of the means of grace, Luther made it a
point to dissociate himself from those subjective theories
of the means of grace which tied the efficacy of the sacraments to the person of the priest or even to that of
the recipient. Such theories had begun "to base baptism
on the holiness of men, though Christ had based it on
his word and commandment." But no one could ever be
sure of his baptism if he had to look into the heart of the
one who baptized him; nor, for that matter, could one's
own state of heart be made the issue. For just as Luther
was contending in this very year for the position that
even unworthy communicants received the true body and
blood of Christ, against all attempts to make the real
presence in the eucharist conditional on faith; so he also
maintained that the baptism of one who did not believe
was "a correct baptism in itself, regardless of whether
or not it was received rightly."[6] Neither the faith of the
priest nor that of the candidate could affect the objective
validity of the sacrament of baptism.

THE ARGUMENT FROM THE NATURAL ORDER

Another parallel between the controversy over infant
baptism and the controversy over the eucharist was the
attention devoted in both of them to the proper place of
reason and of the natural order in theological discourse.
But while the conflict over the eucharist was the occasion
for some of Luther's most violent attacks on "the old
witch, Lady Reason," he found himself contending in
the conflict over infant baptism against those who

spurned any theological argument from the natural order. They repudiated infant baptism, he said, because it made certainty about baptism dependent on the witness of man rather than on the testimony of God. Anyone baptized in infancy had to trust the word of other men. Luther's opponents could throw his own words back at him and ask: "Have you not yourself taught that we should obey God and not man?"[7] Thus he was compelled to clarify what he had meant by the distinction between obeying God and obeying man and in the process to state what place the "natural" testimony of other men occupied in his theology of church structures.

Accurately or inaccurately, Luther associated this denial of the natural order by the Anabaptists with their "intramundane asceticism" and their quasi-monastic repudiation of the structures of the world. Therefore he took the controversy with them as an occasion to affirm the integrity of those structures. In contrast to the Anabaptists' willingness to disrupt marriage, the state, and public order over the issue of rebaptism, Luther's Reformation "not only allows but commands that every estate should remain and be held in honor, and that faith should exercise itself peaceably in love," that is, that faith should not abolish or disrupt, but uphold and sustain, the structures and "estates" of the natural order. Luther attacked the left wing of the Reformation at least partly for being seditious of the secular order and not only for being heretical and schismatic in the spiritual order. Part of his defense of infant baptism, therefore, was also a defense of the natural order, and the argument from reason assumed an unwonted importance in his theology at this point. The conventional assessment of Luther's attitude toward reason has been based on his fulminations against the intrusion of reason into the area of authority that belonged to the word of God. But Luther continually emphasized that reason had a constructive function, also in the work of the theologian as a servant of the word of God.[8] Reason could not tell him what to think, but it could and did tell him how to think.

At least this much is implied in the reply of *Concerning Rebaptism* to the charge that infant baptism was a case of believing man rather than God. For Luther did not base this reply only on an extensive analysis of the biblical evidence, but simultaneously on a series of "natural" analogies in which one believed God by believing man. Without developing a detailed theory, he seems to have meant that the authority of the gospel was mediated through other men, so that the *reductio ad absurdum* of what he took to be the Anabaptist position would be the rejection of any Christian teaching, even of the person and work of Christ and the proclamation of the apostles, simply because it had been transmitted through other men. At this point the transmission of the knowledge given by revelation was of a piece with the transmission of knowledge given to reason. The biblical principle that the testimony of two or three witnesses was evidence trustworthy enough to sustain a fact applied equally to both ways of knowing. One's birth was a work of God, but when one believed the evidence of the witnesses who testified to it, one was believing God through them. The deeds of God were in the public realm and were to be verified in the public realm: "God's works go on so publicly that neither devil nor man can controvert them but every man can so know and declare them as he declares that you are alive. . . . In sum, when any one declares and bears witness to something which is the work of God and which is not the figment of man's imagination, and this can be controverted neither by the devil nor by man, then you are believing God and not man, for it is the work of God which he so publicly discloses that even the devil cannot deny it."[9]

Therefore the biblical command to honor father and mother was reinforced by the evidence of human witnesses that a particular couple were one's parents. The biblical imperative to obey the government took shape through the witness of other men that one was a citizen of this particular realm and was subject to its ruler. Both parental authority and governmental authority were works of God, not merely works of men. But they "went on so publicly" that the experience of other men and the conclusions of reason about that experience could quite legitimately be cited in support of them. Reason agreed with revelation that a man has "to have a mother and father and [is] not sprung from a rock," as Luther said, quoting Homer and Genesis in the same sentence. And it was perfectly legitimate, he maintained in opposition to some Anabaptists, when "St. Paul recognized the heathen poets Aratus and Epimenides and honored their sayings as a word of God." Therefore it was also legitimate to cite the testimony of others about one's baptism. It was an institution commanded by God, as were parenthood and the government. Others testified that baptism had been administered, and by admitting one to the eucharist they showed that they were persuaded both of the fact and of the validity of that baptism. A refusal to accept such testimony was tantamount to a refusal to believe the authority of God.[10]

It would be a mistake to treat this argument from the natural order in isolation. Its context was still the theological and exegetical case which Luther was making in defense of infant baptism. On the other hand, it would also be a mistake to suppose that this argument was no more than a response to the disparagement of the natural order which Luther thought he sensed in the Anabaptist position. The analogies to baptism with which Luther was working in this argument were, significantly, all taken from the doctrine of creation—birth, parenthood, government. The positive evaluation of reason and of the natural order here in *Concerning Rebaptism* was part of Luther's appreciation of the natural good in the creation, a good which sin could not defile and which redemption did not debase. As the Small Catechism of the following year was to say, baptism was not merely plain water;[11] it was more than natural. But that did not make it less than natural, and therefore the argument from the natural order and from reason had a legitimate, though a limited, place in the theological defense of infant baptism.

THE ARGUMENT FROM CONTINUITY

The defense of infant baptism involved Luther not only in a rather surprising assertion of the legitimate place of reason in theological discourse, but also in a defense of traditional structures against the "spiritualism" of the left-wing reformers. During these years he was defending tradition also against his opponents in the eucharistic controversies, who accused him of being "a good papist who believes that there is no wine in the Supper." To this accusation he replied: "Sooner than have mere wine with the fanatics, I would agree with the pope that there is only blood." He claimed to discern a parallel between the position of the one group on infant baptism and the position of the other on the real presence. The former claimed by their rebaptism "to spite the pope and to be free of any taint of the Antichrist," while the latter "want to believe only in bread and wine, in opposition to the pope, thinking thereby really to overthrow the papacy." In both instances a hostility to traditional structures had produced an indifference to the need for continuity and a definition of the Reformation in negative terms. Or, in the words which Luther put into his opponents' mouths, "whatever comes from the pope is wrong. If something goes on in the papacy in a particular way, we must do it some other way."[12]

Such statements seemed to Luther to be drawing not only a false definition of his Reformation, but a false conclusion from its identification of the pope as Antichrist. The pope did indeed demonstrate the aptness of that identification by persecuting, cursing, excommunicating, hounding, burning, and executing unfortunate Christians. Luther was proud that he had come to recognize the papacy as the fulfillment within history of the prophecies of the New Testament about the Antichrist. But it was essential to this recognition that the "man of lawlessness" and "son of perdition" described in those prophecies was to be one who "takes his seat in the temple of God." Far from meaning that "whatever comes from the pope is wrong," therefore, the identification of

the pope as Antichrist meant that "the Christendom
that now is under the papacy . . . has the true Spirit,
gospel, faith, baptism, sacrament, keys, the office of the
ministry, prayer, Holy Scripture, and everything that
belongs to Christendom." From this it even followed
that "we are all still under the papacy," but still more
that a continuity with the Christendom of the papacy was
something to be cultivated rather than spurned. For
"everything that is Christian and good is to be found
[under the papacy] and has come to us from this
source." This meant all of the gifts and marks of the
true church just enumerated, including baptism. If the
papacy, as the seat of Antichrist, "is not a haunt of heretics, but true Christendom," then the conclusion was un-
avoidable that the papacy "must truly have a baptism
which is right beyond any doubt." But that baptism was
infant baptism, now vindicated by the very identification
which had been used to attack it. Thus the pathos that
has always attended the conclusion that the pope was the
Antichrist attended Luther's polemic as well. As he put
it, half-seriously and half-mockingly, "In fact both remain, the Antichrist sits in the temple of God through
the action of the devil, while the temple still is and remains the temple of God through the power of Christ.
If the pope will suffer and accept this dissembling of mine,
then I am and will be, to be sure, an obedient son and
devoted papist, with a truly joyful heart, and take back
everything that I have done to harm him."[13] But in any
event the identification of the pope as Antichrist was an
argument for continuity rather than discontinuity.

Luther found any discontinuity simply inconceivable
which would assert that there had been no baptism for

the thousand years or more when only infant baptism had been practiced. The article of the creed about the church meant that the church would always continue. Yet if its baptism was invalid, the church had been without baptism and was therefore itself invalid. But since infant baptism had been accepted and practiced universally throughout the church, this "gives rise not to the probability that it is wrong, but rather to a strong indication that it is right." By contrast, the sacrificial view of the mass had not been accepted and practiced universally, for among the laymen the mass still remained a sacrament rather than a sacrifice; therefore the argument from continuity did not favor the doctrine that the mass was a sacrifice. Similarly, the argument did not hold in the case of the papacy itself; "for not only has the Eastern church borne testimony against the papacy and opposed it, but so have many subjects of the pope himself." Therefore the authority of the papacy could not claim the sort of unbroken and unopposed continuity that could be cited in support of infant baptism. So deeply impressed was Luther with that continuity that he was willing to formulate a general criterion: "No heresy endures to the end, but always . . . soon comes to light and is revealed as disgraceful." The Bible, the Our Father, and the Apostles' Creed had all met this criterion, having continued from antiquity to the present. The papacy, however, had not; for it "is an innovation and has never been accepted by all Christians."[14] The continuity of the church had been preserved in spite of the papacy, but because of infant baptism. Thus it was evidence for the correctness of infant baptism.

Further support from the continuity of the church

was provided by the empirical evidence in the lives of the saints. There had been genuine saints whose only baptism was infant baptism. To them God had given his great and holy gifts, thus confirming the gift conferred on them in their baptism. If their very baptism had been invalid and an act of disobedience to the divine command, he would not have commended it by these additional blessings. Just as the apostles had established from the gift of the Holy Spirit to the Gentiles that observance of the Mosaic law was not required, so the gift of the Holy Spirit to those baptized in infancy proved that rebaptism was not required. Thus, ironically, Spirit in this instance confirmed Catholic structure. The only specific saint whom Luther named here in *Concerning Rebaptism* was John Hus. In the Large Catechism of 1529 he repeated this argument but expanded the catalogue of the saints: "Since God has confirmed baptism through the gift of his Holy Spirit, as we have perceived in some of the fathers, such as St. Bernard, Gerson, John Hus, and others [who were baptized in infancy], and since the holy Christian church will abide until the end of the world, our adversaries must acknowledge that infant baptism is pleasing to God."[15] Thus the list of "fathers" came to include not only Bernard of Clairvaux, but John Hus and John Gerson, who had been on opposite sides at the Council of Constance. All of them were church fathers; all of them had been baptized in infancy; all had received the Holy Spirit. They gave proof for the continuity of this structure and for its validity.

Yet if the pretensions of the papacy—against which Bernard of Clairvaux, John Hus, and John Gerson had all protested, albeit in quite different ways—were to be rejected, in spite of claims for papal continuity, on the grounds that the papacy was an innovation in the history of the church, the argument from continuity was incomplete without an argument from antiquity. "Our baptism has been of this sort from the beginning of Christianity, and the custom has been to baptize children," Luther asserted. And the antiquity of the usage argued for its retention. Enunciating a principle he had formulated in his defense of Catholic liturgical practice, he declared: "We should not discard or alter what cannot be discarded or altered on clear Scriptural authority." But the first half of this sentence read: "Baptism did not originate with us, but with the apostles." And in the context "baptism" would seem to mean "infant baptism." Elsewhere in *Concerning Rebaptism* Luther did make the claim that infant baptism was not only an ancient usage, but an apostolic one. "Infant baptism," he stated, "derives from the apostles and has been practiced since the days of the apostles." At that point he did not supply any evidence in support of the claim, and was even compelled to admit that "from Scripture we cannot clearly conclude that you could establish infant baptism as a practice among the first Christians after the apostles." But earlier in the treatise he had done so—from St. Augustine: "For St. John in 1 John 2:14 writes to the little children, that they know the Father. And, as St. Augustine writes, infant baptism has come from the apostles." Once more it would appear important not to isolate such a statement from the total context of the argument from continuity, for to do so would be to make it an argument in a circle. But in that context, the claim to antiquity formed part of an affirmation of traditional structures which shifted the burden of proof to the "spiritual" iconoclast. Even in the absence of explicit Scriptural warrant for the practice, "you can well conclude that in our day no one may reject or neglect the practice of infant baptism which has so long a tradition, since God has actually not only permitted it, but from the beginning so ordained that it has not yet disappeared."[16]

THE ARGUMENT FROM THE COVENANT

The argument from continuity was intended to shift the field of battle from the subjective to the objective, so that one did not look at the vagaries of his own faith but at the ordinances of God as given in the church and in its tradition. Yet to fathom the depths of Luther's character as a man and as a reformer, it is essential to recognize that he did not merely refer private faith to the church and its traditional structures, but referred these structures, in turn, to the objective commands and promises of God. As he put it in an axiom in the *Galatians* of 1535, "This is the reason why our theology is certain: it snatches us away from ourselves and places us outside ourselves, so that we do not depend on our own strength, conscience, experience, person, or works, but depend on that which is outside ourselves, that is, on the promise and truth of God, which cannot deceive."[17] Also in the case of infant baptism, this "promise and truth of God, which cannot deceive" proved to be the final ground both of his confidence and of his argument.

It was, in fact, "the very strongest and surest ground," for it rooted baptism not in the fluctuations of human faith and experience but in the foundation of the divine

covenant. The divine covenant was universal in its validity, extending not only to adults and not only to children, but to "all nations." In Matt. 28:19–20 "Christ
commanded us to teach and baptize all heathen, without
exception." The faith of any individual, even of the
strongest Christian, was continually in doubt, and so was
his private experience. The testimony of other Christians
to his baptism was therefore more certain than his own
experience of it would have been. For the devil could
easily have deluded him into supposing that it had been
a dream or an apparition, but he could not so easily de-
lude the entire company of Christian witnesses. Similarly, the covenant of God was a stronger and a surer
foundation for baptism than the faith of the individual,
for faith, too, was a sometime thing. How could one be
sure, even in the case of an adult, that his faith was authentic and sincere? Luther knew personally, from the
bitter experiences of his years of trial, that one could not
be sure that his repentance was authentic and sincere.
He had sought one confession after another, one father
confessor after another, relying on his repentance as he
now found the Anabaptists relying on their faith—and
with the same result, the loss of the very assurance which
the sacrament was intended to provide. The source of
that assurance could not be the subjective state of the individual. In fact, "it happens, indeed it is so in this matter of faith, that often he who claims to believe does not
at all believe; and on the other hand, he who does not
think he believes, but is in despair, has the greatest
faith."[18]

But when one turned from the experience and faith of
man to the command and promise of God, this fluctua-

tion ceased. This was, for Luther, the significance of the parallel between baptism and circumcision. In both cases God had instituted a sign of his covenant by which man could know that God was graciously disposed toward him. Going well beyond the reflections on Old Testament sacraments which we cited from his *Babylonian Captivity* in Chapter 1, Luther said here that God had given circumcision to Abraham and to his descendants as a sign that his covenant with them would endure. Concerning the faith of any particular individual, God had never said anything to anyone, so that one could not rely on faith. But the covenant was based on God's own command, which could not deceive. To this Abraham and his descendants were to look, not to their subjective state. The command was accompanied by the promise that God would be their God. Now if Abraham and his descendants in the people of Israel had the right to look to the command and promise of God as the ground of their covenant with him, it followed *a fortiori* that in the New Testament the command and promise of God were an even surer ground. "This new covenant and sign must be much more effectual and make those a people of God who receive it." But in the New Testament the beneficiary of the command and promise of God was not the nation of Israel, but "all nations." Thus the command and the promise were universal, excluding no nation and no individual from the divine covenant. How then could any individual or any nation be excluded from the sign of the covenant, which was baptism? Only those who excluded themselves by refusing to accept the sign and the covenant could be denied baptism. Otherwise, "if we follow his command and baptize everyone, we leave it to him to be concerned about the faith of those baptized."[19] The gospel was the same for all nations, and therefore for all individuals, including children. Baptism, too, was the same for all, in accordance with the covenant of God, signed in his command to baptize and sealed in his promise.

The command and the promise of God stood because they were the word of God; the covenant stood because it was the work of God. And "when one sees a work of God, one must yield to it and believe it just as one does when one hears his word."[20] That reciprocity between the word of God and the work of God aptly summarizes Luther's case in defense of infant baptism, based as it was on a correlation between the authority of the Bible and the other testimonies from the natural order and from tradition. Luther's opponents on this issue claimed to be applying the priority of the spirit more rigorously than he; they also accused him of inconsistency when he, who had elevated spirit over structure, now proved to be so unequivocal a defender of this particular structure.[21]

We shall be returning to the question of Luther's consistency, but the explanation of his attitude toward infant baptism does not depend upon an answer to this question. We have already noted in Chapter 2 that Luther's graduated scale of sacraments assigned the foremost position to baptism. This position was based on his conviction that in baptism the believer was not the agent, but a passive recipient. Infant baptism reinforced the passivity. Luther could console himself with his baptism in hours of temptation, defying the devil with the cry *"Baptisatus sum!* I have been baptized!"[22] precisely because it had been done *to* him, not *by* him. Infant baptism was undeniably a structure of the papacy, but for Luther it was also, and chiefly, an instrument of the Holy Spirit. It is also a helpful symbol of the character of the man whose Promethean faith changed the course of history. For faith, too, was not first of all a kind of activity or a species of knowledge, but "a free surrender and a joyous wager on the unseen, untried, and unknown goodness of God."[23] In this faith lies the secret of the character of Martin Luther.

5

Church Law and Divine Law
(1530–1531)

As LUTHER developed his defense of infant baptism of
1527–1528, which we have summarized in the preceding
chapter, evidence for the faith of infants, together with
other traditional material, came to his hand from the
Corpus of the Canon Law. Yet on December 10, 1520,
"the entire student body of the University of Wittenberg had been called together at nine o'clock so that the
decretals of the Antichrist might be burned up," and Luther had consigned the *Corpus of the Canon Law* to the
flames, together with other legal and theological books,
including the bull that had excommunicated him. He
took the occasion of his lectures on the psalms the following day to admonish his hearers to beware of "papis-
tic statutes." As an explanation of his action Luther
drew a contrast not merely between spirit and structure,
but between the Spirit of God and the demonic spirit. It
was, Luther said, "on the prompting of the Spirit (I
hope)" that he had burned the books. The canon law, on
the other hand, had been "written in an un-Christian opposition to Christ, by the inspiration of the evil spirit."[1]
Therefore he had burned it with a joyful heart.

Within a decade or so after burning the *Corpus of the Canon Law,* Luther found himself in the position of having to deal, against his will, with moral and legal issues that had been treated in the canon law. Prefacing his treatise *On Marriage Matters* of 1530 with the warning that "I want to do this not as a judge, official, or regent, but by the way of advice, such as I would in good conscience give as a special service to my good friends," he nevertheless cited, after the Bible and the civil law, "the ancient canons and the best points of the spiritual law [i.e., the canon law]."[2] Despite his demurrers, Luther was speaking in a quasi-official capacity when he wrote *On Marriage Matters*—inevitably so, for by 1530 the Reformation had become a movement and he himself had become an institution. For those very reasons, the relation of the Reformation to canon law—and, as we shall see in Chapter 6, also to the sacramental system—may be discerned most clearly in its more official documents. During the same year as Luther's treatise *On Marriage Matters,* his supporters put forward their official defense of the Reformation in the Augsburg Confession, which was followed by a lengthy commentary, the Apology of the Augsburg Confession, written during 1530 and 1531. In the preface to the Apology its author, Philip Melanchthon, stated it as his procedure "to stick as closely as possible to traditional doctrinal formulas."[3] This was true not only for the formulas of dogma, but also for the formulas of canon law, whose role in the Apology is therefore one of the most illustrative chapters in the account of the Reformation's treatment of the institutional structures of the church.

CANON LAW IN THE APOLOGY

The Apology of the Augsburg Confession made the canon law a subject of frequent comment. In fact, it was from this source that it drew its only pun: "The canon commands that priests be suspended; our canonists suspend them all right—not from office but from trees!" Of course, most references to the canon law, including also the one just cited, represented something far more serious than a play on words. When the Apology said, "We are not putting forward an empty quibble,"[4] this applied not only to the point immediately at hand, but to the entire theological enterprise, also to the evaluation of the place of canon law in the church.

At first glance, the reader might conclude that according to the Apology there was no place for canon law in the church. The writings of the moralists and canonists were filled with "labyrinths" and snares. Luther's achievement had been to free "human minds from the labyrinthine confusions and endless disputations of the scholastic theologians and canonists." The same combination of enemies had been identified already in the preface, which charged that "many articles of Christian doctrine . . . lay hidden under all sorts of dangerous opinions in the writings of the monks, canonists, and scholastic theologians." Specifically, it was claimed that the writings of Luther and his followers had corrected "many vicious errors which through the opinions of the scholastics and canonists had overwhelmed the doctrine of penitence." The Apology often linked scholastics and canonists. On the one hand, "the canonists have twisted

ecclesiastical legislations; they did not understand why
the fathers had enacted them." On the other hand, the
same article leveled the accusation at the scholastic
theologians that "from ancient writers they have taken
certain sayings, decrees as it were, and these they quote
in a twisted way."[5] Although the nature and purpose of
the Apology, as a discussion of dogmatic issues, meant
that the scholastics were attacked more frequently and
more vigorously than the canonists, the latter were not
spared.

"Cursed be our opponents, those Pharisees!" With
these words of imprecation the Apology attacked Luther's opponents even for the importance which they
attached to divine law. The term "Pharisee" in Reformation writings was usually directed against the preoccupation with law on the part both of the scholastic
theologians and of the canonists. If this preoccupation
were accepted, "there will be no difference between phil-
osophical or Pharisaic righteousness and Christian righteousness." And when the Apology cited the authority of
the "voice of Christ upbraiding the Pharisees for setting
up traditions contrary to the command of God," it was,
as the context shows, accusing its opponents of defending "their traditions, contrary to the clear command of
God." These legalistic traditions were the principal factor corrupting the vast literature of moral theology and
canon law; but about saving faith in Christ "there is not
a syllable in this heap of constitutions, glosses, summae,
and penitential letters. They say nothing about Christ.
They only recite lists of sins. The greater part deals
with sins against human traditions." Echoing this attack
was the later assertion that "there are huge tomes, even

whole libraries, that do not contain a single syllable
about Christ or faith in him or the good works to be performed in one's calling, but only the traditions together
with interpretations that make them stricter or easier."[6]
It would seem, therefore, that the Apology had nothing
but scorn for the canon law as part of "the abomination
of desolation."

Nevertheless, just as Luther, a decade after burning
the *Corpus of the Canon Law,* was quoting it, though
reluctantly, on questions of marital legislation, so the
Apology was compelled by the polemical situation to
refer to the canon law. Significantly, most of its citations
claimed to find support in canon law for the position of
the reformers, and even those whose import was negative were sometimes counterbalanced by a reference that
seemed more favorable to the Protestant side. There
would seem to be at least thirteen explicit instances in
which the canon law was invoked as part of the argument of the Apology.[7] Of those thirteen instances, more
than half (eight, to be exact) appeared in Article XII
of the Apology, subtitled "Penitence." This is under-
standable not only because the original occasion of Luther's emergence as reformer had been an abuse of the
canon law concerning penance and indulgences, but also
because the concept of guilt had been worked out at
great length in connection with canonical legislation
about the details of specific crimes.

Easily the most productive among these thirteen quotations from church law was one cited in Article VII,
"The Church." Christians were not to lose confidence,
but were to know that "the church will abide" despite all
its trials. The Apology then set down as succinct a sum-

mary as there is anywhere of the contrast between Spirit and structure in Luther's Reformation: "The creed . . . says 'the church catholic' lest we take it to mean an outward government of certain nations. It is, rather, made up of men scattered throughout the world who agree on the gospel and have the same Christ, the same Holy Spirit, and the same sacraments, whether they have the same human traditions or not." And the authority cited in support of this fundamental Reformation position on Spirit and structure was, of all things, the canon law: "The gloss in the *Decrees* says that 'the church in the larger sense includes both the godly and the wicked,' and that the wicked are part of the church only in name and not in fact, while the godly are part of the church in fact as well as in name.' "[8] This skillful use of a formula from the canon law, the most despised of ecclesiastical structures, to vindicate Luther's position makes it clear that by 1530 the official defense of that position sought to affirm what was valid in church structures even as it sought to maintain Luther's demand for the priority of Spirit over structure.

It would not be enough, therefore, merely to give a catalogue and an exegesis of the citations from the canon law in the Apology, for that procedure would miss some of the most important material, much of which appears in the discussion of topics seemingly unrelated to canon law. As the basis for an examination of this material, a passage in Article XV, "Human Traditions," seems to provide a brief statement of the congeries of ideas expressed here and there throughout the Apology; therefore it will also provide us with an outline for our analysis of those ideas:

"We gladly keep the old traditions set up in the church because they are useful and promote tranquility, and we put the best construction on them, excluding the opinion which holds that they justify. Our enemies falsely accuse us of abolishing good ordinances and church discipline. We can truthfully claim that in our churches the public liturgy is more decent than in theirs, and if you look at it correctly *we are more faithful to the canons than our opponents are.*"[9]

STRUCTURES OF DISCIPLINE MAINTAINED

"Our enemies falsely accuse us of abolishing good ordinances and church discipline." The author of the Apology felt entitled to make this plea because, in the total polemical situation of Luther's Reformation as of 1530/31, the defense of structures of discipline and law had become very much the concern of the Lutheran party. "It was insane . . . to try to impose on us the judicial laws of Moses," he said in support of the civil law, vindicating its legitimacy at the same time against its monastic detractors. But in the name of divine law, summarized in the decalogue, the left wing of the Reformation had raised objections not only against the civil law, but also against the canon law. Therefore the effort of the Apology to dissociate its own position from that of the left wing required an affirmation of the legitimacy both of the civil law and of ecclesiastical legislation: "The church has the command to appoint ministers." Under the terms of that command, the church had developed structures of administrative authority. A few paragraphs later, the Apology, without so much as referring to the method of appointment we have outlined in Chapter 2, avowed "our deep desire to maintain the church polity and various ranks of the ecclesiastical hierarchy, although they were created by human authority. We know that the fathers had good and useful reasons for instituting ecclesiastical discipline in the manner described by the ancient canons." It went on to warn that "the cruelty of the bishops is the reason for the abolition of canonical government in some places, despite our earnest desire to keep it."[10] The responsibility for the breakdown of the "good ordinances" and "church discipline" did not rest with the Reformation, but with its opponents.

Nor was the author of the Apology unaware of the practical problems connected with changes in ecclesiastical structures. Near the end of Article XV, "Human Traditions," he summarized the dilemma of coping with those structures: "This subject of traditions involves many difficult and controversial questions, and we know from actual experience that traditions are real snares for consciences. When they are required as necessary, they bring exquisite torture to a conscience that has omitted some observance. On the other hand, their abrogation involves its own difficulties and problems."[11] In these few words there spoke the experience of an entire decade, during which the Reformation movement had begun to come to terms with the pastoral implications of its theology of spirit and structure. When obedient adherence to the institutional structures of the church was demanded as an essential part of Christian loyalty, pastoral problems such as scrupulosity seemed to be an inevitable outcome. But when the structures were swept

aside, this, too, had "its own difficulties and problems,"
as we have seen in Luther's treatment of the priesthood
and monasticism, summarized in Chapters 2 and 3. The
reference to this dilemma was intended to exonerate Luther's followers of the charge that they were abolishing
good ordinances and the structure of ecclesiastical discipline.

Yet this disclaimer of moral responsibility for the
breakdown of the structures of discipline was qualified
by the principle of interpreting them by putting "the best
construction on them, excluding the opinion that they
justify." Such an interpretation of church law was directed against a twofold distortion of divine law: "first,
because they think that outward and civil works satisfy;
and second, because they add human traditions, whose
works they rank above the works of the law."[12] It was a
false estimate of church law to suppose that any works
of man could ever satisfy the divine law, or to blur the
distinction between divine law and church law. The Apology sought to affirm its regard for church law without
falling into either or both of these errors.

On the first count—the supposition that any works
were adequate for justification—there was ultimately no
difference between the works of divine law and the works
of church law; for if "God does not even give his own
law the honor of meriting eternal life," then works in
obedience to church law surely could not merit it. "From
this point of view there is no difference between our traditions and the ceremonies of Moses." Not only were
works in obedience to the ceremonial law excluded from
consideration: no works of law, whether of divine law
or of church law, could merit justification. The supposi-

tion that they could was the "legalistic opinion," which
"clings by nature to the minds of men." And although
this "opinion" used the commands and promises of divine law as a pretext, it served to stimulate the prolifera-
tion of other commands and, inevitably, of other promises. It "has produced and increased many types of
worship in the church, like monastic vows and the abuses
of the mass; someone has always been making up this or
that form of worship or devotion with this view in mind.
To support and increase trust in such works, the scholastics have declared that by necessity . . . God grants
grace to those who do this." There was no denying that
in the writings of certain theologians it had been supposed "that human traditions are devotions necessary
for meriting justification," rather than "outward rules of
discipline, completely unrelated to the righteousness of
the heart or the worship of God." For example, in one of
the passages cited from the canon law it was clear that
various canonical satisfactions had been "instituted for
the sake of church discipline," not "for placating God."
Therefore an interpretation of such ordinances which
"put the best construction on them, excluding the opinion
that they justify" was more faithful to the intention of
their founders; for they had not believed "that this discipline was necessary for the remission either of the guilt
or of the punishment."[13]

If, then, it was "a wicked opinion that we attain to
the forgiveness of sins because of our works," then "the
discerning reader will easily be able to conclude that we
do not merit the forgiveness of sins by monastic works"
nor by obedience to any other man-made structures. Yet
the confusion of church law with divine law was fraught

with many other kinds of danger as well. In the matter
of rites the Roman Catholic reply to the Augsburg Confession demanded that "there is to be no variation in
those that are a matter of faith and have been received
by the universal church," listing among such universal
rites the sacrificial view of the mass, the invocation of
the saints, and fasting. To this the Apology retorted:
"How devout they are! Apostolic rites they want to
keep, apostolic doctrine they do not want to keep." But
even in the area of rites, these protestations that universal, presumably apostolic, rites must be observed
were vitiated by the practice of Latin Christendom in
withholding the chalice from the laity and thus mutilat-
ing a truly universal rite which could claim institution
not merely by the apostles, but by Christ himself. "If
universal ordinances are necessary, why do they change
the ordinance of Christ's supper, which is not human but
divine?" An entire article, both of the Augsburg Confession and of the Apology, discussed "The Lord's Supper
under Both Kinds," invoking, among other authorities,
the Fourth Council of Toledo of 633.[14]

THE LAW OF CELIBACY

The most thoroughly developed formulation of the
contrast between divine law and church law came in
Article XXIII, "Sacerdotal Marriage." The first draft
of this article expressed astonishment that "on this one
issue . . . the canons are enforced so strictly . . . when
in other cases they are often relaxed for various reasons." In an appeal to Charles V, the final draft of the
article petitioned him to resist the demand that "in op-

position to divine law, the law of the nations, and the canons of the councils . . . you dissolve marriages." The love of one sex for the other "is truly a divine ordinance." And therefore "the jurists have said wisely and correctly that the union of man and woman is by natural right. Now, since natural right is unchangeable, the right to contract marriages must always remain. Where nature does not change, there must remain that ordinance which God has built into nature, and human regulations cannot abolish it." It was a fundamental confusion of the relation between church law and divine law to attempt to repeal a law of nature by an ecclesiastical decree. Moreover, "the pontifical regulation also disagrees with the canons of the councils." Here the contrast was between "the ancient canons," which "do not forbid marriage, nor dissolve marriages that have been contracted, though they may remove those from the public ministry who married while in office" and "these new canons," which "do not represent the decision of the synods but the private judgment of the popes." Therefore the Apology could dare to claim: "We do not object to the councils . . . but we do object to the regulations which the Roman pontiffs have set up since the ancient synods and contrary to their authority. The pontiffs show contempt for the authority of the synods while they want others to accept it as sacrosanct."[15]

Even on the issue of priestly celibacy, where the contrast between divine law and church law was the starkest and the most dramatic, the Apology was not content to point out the contrast, but sought to align itself with the canon law against "the new canons." This was evidently part of what was meant by the claim that "if you look at

it correctly, we are more faithful to the canons than our
opponents are." The more specific claim that "in our
churches the public liturgy is more decent than in theirs"
seems to have applied also to church discipline. A little
later Article XV affirmed "that we diligently maintain
church discipline, pious ceremonies, and the good customs of the church." The use of the mass by Luther's
followers was "more frequent and more devout. . . .
[Our] church attendance is greater than theirs." Mass
was celebrated in the Lutheran churches "every Sunday
and on other festivals. . . . We keep traditional liturgical forms, such as the order of the lessons, prayers,
vestments, etc." There was regular preaching of the
word of God and regular instruction of the young in the
rudiments of the faith, but "among our opponents there
is no catechization of the children at all, though even the
canons give prescriptions about it."[16] Here again the
Apology could invoke the authority of the canons in support of the practice of the Protestant churches and in
denunciation of the practice of those who claimed to be
the appointed guardians of canon law.

Discipline, too, was evidence for the claim that "we
are more faithful to the canons." Indeed, "we gladly
keep the old traditions set up in the church because they
are useful and promote tranquility," and these were the
traditions that were conducive to sound discipline. Civil
discipline was important in the secular community, and
"to preserve it [God] has given laws, learning, teaching,
governments, community, and penalties." As we have
noted earlier, the Apology spoke of defending the legitimacy and integrity of this legal, civil discipline against
both the monks and those whom Luther called "the new

monks" on the left wing of the Reformation. For church discipline, too, ordinances were necessary, "especially when they contain a discipline that serves to educate and instruct the people and the inexperienced." These were worthy of being observed "for the sake of tranquility or bodily profit." Even celibacy and similar observances could qualify if they met the stipulation that they "should be praised 'for the sake of discipline and the common weal,' that is, for the discipline of the body and for public morality." They had not been instituted "for the purpose of meriting the forgiveness of sins or righteousness, [but] . . . for the sake of good order and tranquility in the church."[17]

All of this still proceeded as though the issues of doctrine between the churches were discussable and the issues of structure negotiable. In fact, of course, they no longer were. But for the purposes of our investigation it is even more significant that by 1530–1531 Luther's movement had begun to come to terms with the need for church structures. The naïve supposition that such structures were always an obstacle to the life of the Spirit had given way to the recognition that they could be a positive channel for the Spirit. Even canon law apparently could perform a positive function, provided that it was held within properly prescribed limits and not given credit for justification. Thus, when its structures "are required as necessary, they bring exquisite torture to a conscience that has omitted some observance. On the other hand, their abrogation involves its own difficulties and problems." In the Apology of the Augsburg Confession, Luther's Reformation attempted to set down a theory of institutional structures that avoided both those extremes, for Luther had come to believe that this was the only way for not only ecclesiastical structures, but order and continuity to be preserved. What this desire for order and continuity means in the interpretation both of Luther's own character and of the crisis of the Reformation, we shall seek to determine in the Epilogue to this book.

6

The Sacramental System (1537)

THE SLASHING attack upon the sacramental system in *The Babylonian Captivity of the Church,* summarized in Chapter 1, was written by a priest who had been so overwhelmed with awe while celebrating his first mass that he was scarcely able to finish the celebration. Taken by itself, *The Babylonian Captivity* would certainly seem to justify the conclusion of Adolf von Harnack that Luther "cut the root of the whole catholic notion of the sacraments."[1] Nothing more vigorously articulates Luther's character as reformer and theologian than this bold and single-minded defiance of the sacramental system in which he had been reared and into which he had been ordained. Yet during the remaining quarter-century of his life, the question of the sacraments was repeatedly forced upon his attention, both by the tasks he faced in the creation of structures for evangelical Christianity and by his controversies, most of which concerned the sacraments and the means of grace: with Andrew Carlstadt, John Oecolampadius, Ulrich Zwingli, and Martin Bucer over the real presence in the eucharist; with the Anabaptists over infant baptism; with John Agricola over the preaching of the law.

It would seem, therefore, that Luther's mature per-

spective on the sacraments as structures through which
the grace of God was mediated belongs to any effort at
an assessment of his views on spirit and structure. He
himself and his colleagues seem to have thought so. For
after reaffirming the confession of the orthodox faith
concerning God, man, and Jesus Christ in Articles I, II,
and III, and defining the doctrine of justification by
grace through faith in Article IV, the Augsburg Confession went on in Article V to declare: "To obtain such
faith God instituted the office of the ministry, that is,
provided the gospel and the sacraments. Through these,
as through means, he gives the Holy Spirit."[2] Although
later editions of the confession gave this article the title
"The Office of the Ministry," there would have been
good reason to call it "The Means of Grace" or even
"The Sacramental System." Its position in the sequence
of articles suggests the function of the sacramental system as the link connecting the "doctrine of the gospel"
with the life of the Christian and of the church. In this
summary of Luther's reinterpretation of the sacramental
system, as in other articles, the Augsburg Confession
was consciously setting its view of Spirit and structure
into opposition with both Roman Catholicism and the
left wing of the Reformation. Explicitly it condemned
the separation of the Holy Spirit from the mediating
structures of grace, as maintained by "the Anabaptists
and others who teach that the Holy Spirit comes to us
through our own preparations, thoughts, and works,
without the external word of the gospel." But the Augsburg Confession was no less explicit in attacking the
identification of Spirit and structure by "those who teach
that the sacraments justify by the outward act."[3]

To be sure, Luther did not write the Augsburg Confession, but his Schwabach Articles, one of its sources, had contained a similar formulation. And a few years later, when the Reformation faced the possibility that a reform council, so long postponed, might finally be convoked to deal with the issues it had raised, John Frederick, the Elector of Saxony, instructed Luther to draw up "your opinion about what and how much it is possible to concede and yield . . . and what to demand and insist upon."[4] Luther's response to that request was the composition of the so-called Smalcald Articles of 1537. Although they are divided and subdivided into "parts" and "articles," the Smalcald Articles are not arranged in any precise sequence. Nevertheless, they do contain the most trenchant statement from Luther's later years of his eventual perspective on the sacramental system: "The gospel . . . offers counsel and help against sin in more than one way, for God is surpassingly rich in his grace: first, through the spoken word, by which the forgiveness of sin (the peculiar office of the gospel) is preached to the whole world; second, through baptism; third, through the holy sacrament of the altar; fourth, through the power of the keys; and finally, through the mutual conversation and consolation of brethren."[5]

THE WORD OF GOD AS SACRAMENT

To understand either Luther's theology or his character, it is essential to come to terms with what he meant by the word of God. Throughout his life he preached and reflected on the story of the temptation of Jesus by Satan (Matt. 4:1–11). Christ's secret weapon in that temptation was also the weapon with which Luther armed himself: "It is written, 'Man shall not live by bread alone, but by every word that proceeds from the mouth of God.' " Therefore the fundamental form of the means of grace was "the spoken word, by which the forgiveness of sin (the peculiar office of the gospel) is preached to the whole world." The "living voice of the gospel" was constitutive of any other mediating structure of grace.

Perhaps one reason for the indifference to the technicalities of ministerial continuity which we have noted in Chapter 2 was this emphasis on the centrality of preaching. For Luther's favorite term for the office of the ministry was, as we have seen, not "priesthood"; it was "the office of preaching." Few theological disputes have been carried on with more vehemence and less clarity than the controversy over what constitutes a sacrament. Luther recognized that every definition must be arbitrary, as Chapter 1 has indicated. But there would be good reason to maintain that Luther elevated the preaching of the word of God to the status of a sacrament, indeed, that in a sense he made it the sacrament on which all the other sacraments depended. To Luther this did not mean, as it did to some of his contemporaries, that the other sacraments were no more than various forms of preaching; as we shall see, they were "visible words of God," yet they were more than that. But it did mean that just as "Jesus came . . . preaching the gospel of God" (Mark 1:14), so he had commanded his church to preach the same gospel and had attached the promise of his grace to its preaching. "For God has decreed that no one can or will believe or receive the Holy Spirit without that gospel which is preached or taught by word of mouth."[6]

Luther found both religious comfort for his own faith and theological support for this doctrine in the words of the apostle Paul: "So faith comes from what is heard, and what is heard comes by the preaching of Christ" (Rom. 10:17). From his pioneering *Lectures on Romans* of 1515–1516 to his *Lectures on Genesis* of 1535–1545, which he himself called his "swan song," these words served him as the key to the meaning of faith through proclamation.[7] There are passages in Luther's writings where the preaching and hearing of the word of God threatened to make the church a kind of schoolroom by reducing the worship of the church to its didactic function; there are others in which the proclamation of the word threatened to become as automatic as the sacraments had been in late medieval theory. But at its center the idea of faith through what is heard was an appropriation of the biblical image of "the speaking of the name" as the means by which the power of the demons was broken and the lordship of the Creator was restored. As the discussion in Chapter 3 has made clear, there was a dialectical relation between law and gospel, and "the word" was a word of both judgment and forgiveness. Luther insisted that the proclamation of the living word of the gospel was jeopardized when the law was abused: "in the first place, by all the self-righteous and the hypocrites, who imagine that men are justified by the law. . . . In the second place, the law is abused by those who want to excuse Christians from it altogether. . . . In the third place, the law is abused also

by those who, when they feel its terrors, do not understand that these are to last only until Christ."[8]

A related dialectic was that between the gospel as
message and the gospel as means. In the preface to his
translation of the New Testament of 1522, Luther defined "gospel" as "a Greek word [which] means in
Greek a good message, good tidings, good news, a good
report, which one sings and tells with gladness."[9] "Gospel" in Luther's usage was sometimes virtually identical
with "grace" and at other times virtually identical with
"proclamation of grace." In fact, some such distinction
would seem to be necessary to understand the words
from the Smalcald Articles just quoted; for when Luther
spoke of "the gospel, which offers counsel and help
against sin *in more than one way*" and then went on to
refer to "the spoken word" as one such way, "gospel"
would appear to refer primarily to "grace" or "grace
communicated," while "the spoken word" would appear
to be used for the proclamation, which Luther elsewhere
called "gospel." A crucifix or a stained glass window
could be a medium for the gospel by being a "visible
word," i.e., a representation of the message of the gospel; but that did not put it on a level with baptism or the
eucharist, which conveyed the gospel by being channels
of divine grace.

Another problem in Luther's identification of "the
spoken word" as a means of grace is the relation between the spoken word and the written word, between
preaching and the Bible. Sometimes he contrasted the
spoken word with the written, much to the disadvantage
of the latter; sometimes he did call the Bible "the word

of God." But it is anachronistic to treat these lines of thought as mutually exclusive. Both Luther's devotional life and his practice as a preacher and expositor make it clear that the Bible as the written form of the word was the source from which preaching as the oral form had to be drawn and by which it had to be evaluated, but that the Bible pointed behind itself to the prophetic and apostolic preaching and beyond itself to the continued proclamation of the church. To be Christian, the preaching of the church had to be faithful to Scripture; but to be faithful to Scripture, the church had to preach. As the apostles had based their oral proclamation on the written word of the Old Testament, so the written word of the New Testament became a means of grace by being transposed into preaching.[10]

THE WORD OF GOD IN BAPTISM

After listing the ways in which the gospel offered counsel and help against sin, Luther went on to speak of baptism, which he defined as "nothing else than the word of God in water, commanded by the institution of Christ; or as Paul says, 'the washing of water with the word'; or again, as Augustine puts it, 'The word is added to the element and it becomes a sacrament.'" The polarity of this definition becomes evident from the polemic following it, which condemned, on the one hand, those who ascribed some sort of spiritual power to the water and, on the other hand, those who based the function of baptism as a means of grace on the arbitrary decree of

God. Both positions, in effect, ignored the connection between washing and the word of God.[11] This was an effort by Luther to dissociate his position from several of the alternatives that had developed in medieval theology.

In Luther's own day, however, other alternatives had arisen, partly, so they said, as an aftermath to his own elevation of spirit over structure and sacrament. Claiming to carry out consistently Luther's own protest against medieval sacramentalism, the left wing of the Reformation maintained that the primacy of faith implied the exclusion not only of works and merits, but also of the mediating structures of grace, from the process of salvation. In this respect, though not in others, Zwingli had displayed some affinities with the very Anabaptists against whom he contended. Baptism was the special target of the Anabaptist attack, which argued "that faith alone saves and that works and external things contribute nothing to this end." This argument, Luther replied, failed to recognize "that faith must have something to believe," and that therefore "faith clings to the water and believes it to be baptism in which there is sheer salvation and life, not through the water . . . but through its incorporation with God's word and ordinance and the joining of his name to it."[12] Thus Luther maintained, both against Roman Catholicism and against Anabaptism, that his view of the relation of spirit and structure did not exclude the structure of means of grace, but actually required it. Precisely because man could not contribute to his own salvation by his works, God took the initiative in the mediating structures of grace, and specifically in baptism, to convey his Spirit.

The key to this understanding of baptism was Luther's stress upon the implications of the command and the promise of God. As we have noted in Chapter 4, baptism was "the word of God in water, *commanded by the institution of Christ.*" This could mean simply that one submitted oneself to the ordinance and institution of God, neither understanding nor attempting to understand the meaning of baptism, but unquestioningly accepting the divine command. Baptism—as well as the other sacraments—would then be a part of Christian ethics, the affirmation of the confidence that the will of God is good and wise altogether even though we do not comprehend its purpose. But so unsacramental a view of baptism would certainly not do justice to Luther's doctrine. Even the young Luther stressed both the command and the promise of God in baptism, thus finding reassurance and hope in the covenant by which God had bound himself to baptism. The command and the promise articulated in the institution of baptism by Christ and confirmed by the practice of the apostolic church in the Book of Acts meant that the church was not forced to rely on its own resources after the ascension of Christ. It could be assured that the withdrawal of his physical presence did not mean the withdrawal of the grace of God. For by commanding the apostles to baptize and by promising that he would be with them and their successors to the end of the age, Christ had assured the continuity of the Christian church throughout human history and beyond it.[13] That continuity was also the fundamental leitmotiv of Luther's defense of the practice of infant baptism, analyzed in Chapter 4.

THE EUCHARIST AS STRUCTURE
AND SACRAMENT

Although Luther was involved in controversy with the Anabaptists over the sacramental nature of baptism as a means of grace and over the propriety of infant baptism, the most vigorous conflict over the sacramental system in his career was the conflict (or, rather, the series of conflicts) in which he defended his doctrine of the eucharist. As the doctrine of the eucharist had probably contributed more than any other doctrine to the development of the traditional definitions of the term "sacrament" during the Middle Ages,[14] so it was probably in his struggle to articulate and defend the doctrine of the eucharist that Luther was forced to state his definition of the sacraments as mediating structures of grace with the greatest force and precision.

For it was that definition that was at stake in the eucharistic controversy. The line of battle was indeed drawn at the issue of the real presence, but the war was being fought over the issue of the grace of God and the means and structures by which that grace was mediated. Luther himself claimed that his insistence upon the real presence of the body and blood of Christ in the eucharist was inseparable from his insistence that the salvation of man was achieved solely by the grace of God, without human cooperation, and that man appropriated this grace solely by faith. On the other hand, it is easy to elevate his occasional and, for him, quite guarded statements about such metaphysics into more of an ontological theory than he himself seems to have intended.

There is at least some historical basis for maintaining that when Luther was confronted with a position that was less precise than his own about the real presence in the eucharist, but was no less firm than his about the doctrine of grace, he was willing to be charitable and patient. Thus in relation both to Martin Bucer, in the consideration of the Wittenberg Concord of 1536, and to the Unity of Bohemian Brethren, in the consideration of their *Confession* of 1535 which he published in 1538, Luther acted in a manner quite different from his attitude toward Zwingli.[15]

At least part of the reason for the difference was Luther's assertion, formulated in the course of an evaluation of the various theories about the eucharist prevalent among the Hussites, that the most dangerous heresy of all in the doctrine of the eucharist was that which regarded it as "a sacrifice and a good work." In *The Babylonian Captivity,* as we have noted in Chapter 1, he had called this view "the third captivity." Mediating structure of grace though it unquestionably was, the eucharist did not confer grace in the sense of being a repetition of Calvary. The original provocation for Luther's assertion was the elaborate structure into which the mass had evolved, based on the theory that the mass was an "unbloody sacrifice" that availed as a means of obtaining the grace of God. This Luther rejected with unremitting vehemence all his life. But he also recognized that there was a subtle but profound affinity between this equation of sacrifice with sacrament and the rejection of all structure in the name of the Holy Spirit. Despite their obvious differences, both views seemed to him to emphasize human initiative and responsibility in the sacrament at the cost of the priority of divine grace. The sacrificial idea of the mass still made the eucharist a mediating structure of grace, but it did so by a fundamental distortion of what Luther took to be the meaning of "grace"; the other extreme, in Luther's judgment, vitiated its repudiation of the mass by setting forth an understanding of the grace-relation and therefore of the sacrament that was still centered in man.[16] The eucharist was a means of grace, but not in either of these senses.

This method of defining by means of a "yes-but" appears throughout Luther's controversies over the eucharist, for he attacked his opponents' teachings not so much for being wrong in themselves as for being inadequate. That is, he accused them of attributing the primary significance of the sacrament to one aspect of eucharistic theology and of neglecting that on which it depended, the doctrine of the real presence and its corollary, the doctrine of the means of grace. When, for example, Carlstadt assigned central importance to the act of remembrance in the eucharist, Luther wrote: "He gives . . . remembrance the power to justify, as faith does. The proof he gives is, he says, that it is written that they have done this 'in remembrance of me.' What think you? It is written that they have done it 'in remembrance of me.' Therefore such remembrance justifies. . . . Such remembrance does not justify, but . . . they must first be justified who would preach, proclaim, and practice the outward remembrance of Christ."[17] Remembrance did not justify, nor did it cause Christ to be present. But because Christ had commanded the celebration of the Lord's Supper and had promised that his body and his blood would be present, the remembrance of his words and deeds was an integral part of the total celebration: it was a means of grace and therefore a remembrance, not *vice versa.*

There was a similar connection between the sacrament as a means of grace and the sacrament as a communion. In the controversy with Zwingli, Luther came to place less emphasis on the idea of communion than he had earlier. He had said in 1519: "The significance or purpose of this sacrament is the fellowship of all saints, whence it derives its common name *synaxis* or *communio,* that is, fellowship; and *communicare* means to take part in this fellowship, or as we say, to go to the sacrament." It would be difficult to duplicate this statement from the controversies of the late 1520's and following.[18] For Luther, the Lord's Supper was not less than a communion or fellowship; it was that, but it was more. As we shall note later, the common life shared by Christians in the church also performed the function of a mediating structure of grace, and the fellowship in the Lord's Supper had its share in that function. But Luther regarded it as false to reduce the means of grace in the eucharist to the horizontal dimension. In fact, the action of God through the word and the sacraments, as means of grace, called the communion of Christians into being. Thus the eucharist was a means of grace and therefore a communion.

As a means of grace, the eucharist was also a powerful symbol: more than a symbol, but not less. In his presentation of baptism in the Small Catechism of 1529, Luther included a question on baptism as a symbol: "What does such baptizing with water signify?" but only after an explanation of baptism as a means of grace. Although no similar discussion appears in the Small

Catechism's presentation of the eucharist, Luther never ceased reflecting and speaking about the symbolism of the eucharist, as his sermons show. Not only the eucharist, but the whole creation was a mask and a symbolic bearer of the meaning of God's concern for the world. The grass and the trees became sacramentals: "The sun preaches this to you every day"; and "a little finch, which can neither speak nor read, is [one's] theologian and master in the Scriptures."[19] But that did not make the eucharist simply part of a sacramental universe or only a special illustration of a general principle. It was this, but it was more.

THE SACRAMENT OF ABSOLUTION

With the discussion of baptism and the eucharist we come to the end of the list of sacraments as Protestants have traditionally counted them. As we have already noted, however, Luther did not make as much a point of this as did some later Protestants. Chapter 1 has shown that even in *The Babylonian Captivity* he did not simply assert that "there are, strictly speaking, but two sacraments in the church of God—baptism and the bread," but also suggested in the very same context that "prayer, the word, and the cross" were among the "things which it might seem possible to regard as sacraments." Above all, he remained willing to speak of absolution—his usual term was "the power of the keys"— as a sacrament; and in keeping with his practice, the Apology of the Augsburg Confession, whose conservative attitude toward church structures we have examined in Chapter 5, declared that "the genuine sacraments

. . . are baptism, the Lord's Supper, and absolution (which is the sacrament of penitence)."[20]

But the question of whether or not absolution should be called a sacrament could easily become a quibble. For our purposes it is more important to note that there was no question at all about the appropriateness of its being called a means of grace. In their exposition of the list of means of grace the Smalcald Articles went on to call the power of the keys "a function and power given to the church by Christ to bind and loose sins. . . . Since absolution or the power of the keys, which was instituted by Christ in the gospel, is a consolation and help against sin and a bad conscience, confession and absolution should by no means be allowed to fall into disuse in the church, especially for the sake of timid consciences and for the sake of untrained young people who need to be examined and instructed in Christian doctrine." These words express the deeply pastoral concern at work throughout Luther's mature attitude toward the mediating structure of grace, as well as his pedagogical interest in the Christian nurture of the young. Absolution had a special role, for it was the personal application of the gospel to the individual. As Luther had said already in 1519, "If you believe the word of the priest when he absolves you . . . then your sins are assuredly absolved also before God, before all angels and all creatures."[21] As we have noted in Chapter 1, this was not because he believed that private confession was divinely instituted in the same sense as baptism and the eucharist, but because he recognized the need for it in the Christian life, even in the Christian life of the Reformation churches.

Because of this recognition of need, Luther urged

throughout his career that private confession and personal absolution be retained in the churches. As part of the reformatory program set forth in Chapter 1, Luther had expected that private confession and absolution would be retained even after such structures as sacerdotal authority (discussed in Chapter 2), the monastic orders (treated in Chapter 3), and the canon law (analyzed in Chapter 5), all of which undergirded private confession, had been replaced by an evangelical churchmanship. In this expectation he was mistaken. For private confession was one of the many structures which, while retained by Luther and his colleagues, eventually collapsed.[22] So strong was the antipathy to medieval abuses and so violent the reaction that only a few of Luther's descendants managed to cling to personal absolution as a vestigial remnant of Luther's teaching.

For some reason or other, Protestantism, in Luther's phrase, "learned [the lesson of freedom] only too well," managing to keep a firmer hold on Luther's rejection of the identification of spirit and structure than on the positive reinterpretation of the structures. The implications of this will claim our attention again in the Epilogue to this book. Two objections to the medieval structure of penance and absolution predominated in Luther's polemics. One was the rejection of the demand that in private confession sins be enumerated. "The enumeration of sins," wrote Luther in the Smalcald Articles, "should be left free to everybody to do or not as he will." This was directed against the canonical legislation of the Fourth Lateran Council of 1215, which had required that ". . . every believer of either gender, after he has arrived at the age of discretion, should himself confess all his sins faithfully at least once a year to his own priest." But it was directed even more against the abuses in the pastoral care of medieval Catholicism, for Luther's character and his convictions had been shaped by his personal experience that legalism among the clergy and indifference among the laity were the twin effects of the confusion between the law and the gospel. In the reconstitution of parochial life undertaken by the reformers, notably in the visitations of the late 1520's, the scars left by these abuses had become evident. What had been intended as a means of grace had become instead "nothing but tyranny," resulting either in the despair of the suicide or the smugness of the hypocrite. Both as a priest and as a penitent, Luther had come to know at first hand the psychological as well as the theological therapy that could come in confession, but he had good reason from the same experience to oppose a compulsory enumeration of sins.[23]

He had, if anything, even better reason, also from his personal experience, to oppose the tyranny of the clergy in confession. The power of the keys had been given to the entire church, not only to the bishops and priests. As Chapter 2 points out, the fundamental meaning of the universal priesthood of all believers was not that every Christian was his own priest, but that every Christian was his brother's priest; not individualism, but mutual responsibility was its basic intent. And one of the ways for the believer to exercise his priesthood toward a fellow Christian was by acting as his confessor. As Luther said in his most far-reaching attack on the notion of the priesthood (which we have outlined in Chapter 2), "the keys belong to the whole church and to each of its members, as regards both their authority and their various uses. Otherwise we do violence to the words of Christ, in which he speaks to all without qualification or limitation." Yet the priesthood of believers did not exclude the clergy, as though everyone were a priest but they. Luther's manuals of penitence and his exhortations to confession proceeded on the assumption that the public exercise even of private absolution would be carried out by the minister, who would thus apply to the individual the same proclamation of forgiveness that was the essential content of his preaching to the entire congregation. But in the individual application as well as in the general announcement of the word, the minister acted in the name of the church, which was both the product of the means of grace—"the daughter who is born from the word . . . not the mother of the word," in Luther's phrase—and the dispenser of the means of grace to others.[24]

THE CHURCH A MEDIATING STRUCTURE OF GRACE

Therefore it would not be a distortion to say that in Luther's theology the church itself was a mediating structure of grace, for the final item on his list of means of grace was "the mutual conversation and consolation of brethren." The statement of the creed, "I believe in the church," was always an integral factor of his personal faith and of his theology. Later Protestant individualism has failed to do justice to his doctrine of the church and has represented Luther in a false light. But Luther continued to declare throughout his life that the witness and the support of the church were indispensable. He said in the Small Catechism that it was "in this Christian church" that God "daily and abundantly forgives all my sins."[25] The church was not an afterthought in Luther's faith. As we have had occasion to note several times in this book, the doctrine of the church was fundamental to Luther's entire attitude toward the structures of the church. Because he thought of the church as he did, he took the attitude he did toward its structures.

The synonym for "the church" here in the Smalcald Articles was "the brethren." For a former monk this term was bound to have all sorts of connotations. Chapter 3 has pointed out that monasticism was an issue in Luther's thought for many years. Luther's description of the true Christian congregation represents something of an afterglow of the monastic ideal. Set apart from the world in order to serve the world, the congregation of real and earnest Christians would be made up of those who "profess the gospel with hand and mouth." They "should sign their names and meet alone in a house somewhere to pray, to read, to baptize, to receive the sacrament, and to do other Christian works." Although this ideal proved to be structurally unattainable, "brotherly troth and fervent love" continued to be part of Luther's picture of the church. Especially was this true of his picture of the church as a mediating structure of grace, where "counsel and help against sin" were provided. For "where judging or rebuking is necessary, those should do it who have the office and the commission to do it . . . or a brother with a brother alone, on the basis of a brotherly love that bears and corrects the neighbor's faults."[26]

This was the real meaning of confession and absolution, when brethren confessed their sins to brethren and received the assurance of the forgiveness of sins from them. It was "mutual" because sin was universal and the need for the mercy of God was a sign of the true church. In defining the "true church" by its need for mercy rather than by its possession either of legitimate institutional structures or of empirically verifiable holiness in the Spirit, Luther went beyond the tension of Spirit and structure to the very meaning of grace and forgiveness: "The true church is the one which prays . . . fervently: 'Forgive us our debts as we forgive our debtors' (Matt. 6:12). The church is made up of those who move forward in the process of becoming holy. . . . You must not look for a church in which there are no blemishes and flagrant faults, but for one where the pure word of God is present, where there is the right administration of the sacraments, and where there are people who love the word and confess it before men."[27]

Luther was too aware of the "blemishes and flagrant faults" both in the life of the church and in his own character ever to claim that a community of pure saints could be found on earth or to base the validity of the sacraments upon such a claim. On the other hand, his attack in *The Babylonian Captivity* on a sacramental system divorced from the word of God made any such system equally unacceptable as a solution of the dilemma. But in sacraments that were simultaneously rooted in the word and embodied in the church, sacraments that acted as mediating channels of the unmerited mercy of God, he found true structures of the Holy Spirit; and in this sense he claimed to be more loyal to the sacramental

system than his opponents were. In the Epilogue to this
volume we shall turn now to the question of "Spirit in
Structure," to determine the pattern of Luther's attitude
toward the institutional structures of the church, and thus
to probe a little more deeply the mystery of his "character in crisis."

Epilogue: Spirit in Structure

MARTIN LUTHER developed his character in the crisis of Christian institutions. The Luther of Chapter 1 was a man in his thirties, who had emerged as a reformer only two or three years before. The Luther of Chapter 6 was a man in his fifties, who would be dead in less than ten years. There are times when his development reminds one of the sorcerer's apprentice in Goethe's poem (and in Disney's *Fantasia*), who, having learned the magical formula that commands the broom to carry water but not the formula that makes it stop, cries out: "I summoned the spirits, but now I can't get rid of them!"

The development of Luther's character was a quest for certainty. In the radicalism of 1520, as we have seen in Chapter 1, he could claim to be announcing publicly "the counsel I have learned under the Spirit's guidance." But as we have also seen, by the later 1530's his quest for certainty had taken the form of asserting: "This is the reason why our theology is certain: it snatches us away from ourselves and places us outside ourselves." When "structure" meant the objective authority of an ecclesiastical institution arbitrarily enforced from without, Luther opposed it in the name of the freedom of the Spirit—the old Luther no less than the young. When

"spirit" meant the free-floating subjectivity of an individual who had "swallowed the Holy Spirit, feathers
and all," Luther opposed it in the name of the gift of
grace—the young Luther no less than the old. It was
as a young man that Luther had learned, in the bitter
experience of his guilt and penance, how unreliable a
foundation for certainty his own subjective feelings
could be. And he was no longer a young man when he
still felt able to boast that he, too, "had been in the
Spirit and seen the Spirit, perhaps even more of it (if it
comes to boasting of one's flesh) than those fellows with
all their boasting will see in a year."[1]

It is, therefore, only partially valid to contrast Luther's character as a young man with his character in
later years, as when one scholar maintains that "between
the years 1519 and (about) 1523 Luther [took] a step
of advance that had the promise in it of more thorough
reforms" than he actually carried out, while another declares that "we take our stand only on the later, mature,
and more developed Luther."[2] Both Luther's character
and his development in the crisis of the Reformation
were more complex than such simple contrasts would
suggest. But it is clear from our study that the development of his character came to terms only gradually with
his continuing reliance on some sort of structure for the
Spirit—but not just any sort of structure, nor any sort of
Spirit.

There is little use in speculating about what Luther's
character might have been or become if it had not been
for the crisis of the Reformation. He was, as we have
said, "a young man on the way up." But it was the crisis
of the Reformation that made him know himself with an

accuracy, and speak of himself with a candor, rarely
matched in the character of great men. More specifically,
it was the crisis of Christian institutions which taught
him to see himself with that unique combination of self-
assertion and self-depreciation which was so characteris-
tic of him.[3] "While I was drinking beer," he would say,
"God reformed the church." And he meant it. As Luther
had occasion to know from personal experience, those
structures of the church which gave one the feeling that
one was in control of things—structures such as monasticism, the papacy, or a baptism based on the personal
profession of one's faith—were a temptation of Satan
and a mark of Antichrist. But he also knew from profound introspection and honest self-examination that
those structures of the church through which the unmerited goodness of God was communicated—even if,
as in the case of private confession and perhaps also of
infant baptism, their divine institution was not beyond
question—were means of grace.

This insight is basic both to Luther's theology and to
his personal character. One does not understand Martin
Luther until one recognizes above all that he was sus-
tained neither by the support of others nor by his confidence in himself. He had made his own the words of
the apostle Paul in 1 Cor. 4:3–4: "With me it is a very
small thing that I should be judged by you or by any
human court. I do not even judge myself. It is the Lord
who judges me." Not the "heteronomous" authority of
any human court or ecclesiastical structure, however
venerable its continuity might be; nor the "autonomous"
authority of Martin Luther, however filled with the
Spirit he might be; but the "theonomous" authority of

God as he had acted in Christ to redeem the world and as he communicated himself in the means of grace—this theonomy, "Spirit-determined and Spirit-directed," in which "Spirit fulfils spirit instead of breaking it—"⁴ was the ground of Luther's confidence and the key to his character.

Luther was looking for certainty about the grace of God; today we would have to be certain first about the God of grace. From today's vantage point the differences between Luther and his various opponents, as set forth in the preceding chapters, seem far less significant than the profound and often unexpressed assumptions which they all shared, but which are not shared by the great majority of men in the twentieth century. Yet if one of the differences between Luther's character and that of men today is the change that has come in the very possibility of speaking about a transcendent reality "out there" which the structures of grace were thought to mediate to men, it may be necessary to reverse the traditional order of things. To come to terms with Luther's character in the midst of the crisis of the Reformation, we have to begin not with his view of the "out there" at all, but with his view of the "down here," proceeding from structure to Spirit and not from Spirit to structure. Such a procedure is indeed, the one he himself urged and followed:

"I say of the right hand of God: although this is everywhere, as we may not deny, still because it is also nowhere, as has been said, you can actually grasp it nowhere, unless for your benefit it binds itself to you and summons you to a definite place. This God's right hand does, however, when it enters into the humanity of

Christ and dwells there. There you surely find it, otherwise you will run back and forth throughout all creation, groping here and groping there yet never finding, even though it is actually there; for it is not there for you. . . . He himself gives meaning to the bread for you, by his word, bidding you to eat him."[5]

ABBREVIATIONS

BC   *The Book of Concord,* translated by Theodore G. Tappert, Jaroslav Pelikan, Robert H. Fischer, and Arthur C. Piepkorn. Philadelphia, 1959.

Bek.   *Die Bekenntnisschriften der evangelisch-lutherischen Kirche.* 2nd ed.; Göttingen, 1952.

LW   *Luther's Works* (American Edition), edited by Jaroslav Pelikan and Helmut T. Lehmann. St. Louis and Philadelphia, 1955 ff.

StL   *Dr. Martin Luthers Sämmtliche Schriften.* St. Louis, 1880 ff.

WA   *D. Martin Luthers Werke.* Weimar, 1883 ff. *Briefe (WA Br). Deutsche Bibel (WA DB).*

WML *Works of Martin Luther.* Philadelphia, 1915 ff.

NOTES

PROLOGUE: CHARACTER IN CRISIS

[1] *The Freedom of a Christian, WA* 7, 37 (*LW* 31, 370); *To the Christian Nobility of the German Nation Concerning the Reform of the Christian Estate, WA* 6, 414 (*LW* 44, 138).

[2] Preserved Smith, *Martin Luther* (2nd ed.; New York, 1911), p. xxi.

[3] I have, for example, benefited greatly from the materials collected in Peter Ratkos (ed.), *Dokumenty k baníckemu povstaniu na Slovensku (1525–1526)* (Bratislava, 1957), dealing with the uprising of Slovak miners during the age of the Reformation.

[4] Erik H. Erikson, *Young Man Luther. A Study in Psychoanalysis and History* (New York, 1957); on John Osborne's *Luther,* cf. my review in *Christianity and Crisis,* XXIII, 21 (December 9, 1963), 228–229.

CHAPTER 1. SPIRIT VERSUS STRUCTURE (1520)

[1] *The Babylonian Captivity of the Church, WA* 6, 497–573 (*LW* 36, 11–126). Cf. L. K. Shook, (ed.), *Theology of Renewal,* II, *Renewal of Religious Structures* (Montreal, 1968), 21–41.

[2] *WA* 6, 499 (*LW* 36, 15); *WA* 6, 508 (*LW* 36, 29).

[3] Seneca, *Epistles,* 89, 9; Brooke F. Westcott, *The Gospel of Life* (London, 1892), p. 256, quoted in *The Oxford English Dictionary,* X (Oxford, 1933), 1165.

[4] *WA* 6, 560 (*LW* 36, 107); *WA* 6, 561 (*LW* 36, 108).

[5] *WA* 6, 530 (*LW* 36, 62); *WA* 6, 517 (*LW* 36, 43); *WA* 6, 573 (*LW* 36, 125).

[6] *WA* 6, 540 (*LW* 36, 76); *WA* 6, 534 (*LW* 36, 68); *WA* 6, 531 (*LW* 36, 64).

[7] *WA* 6, 502 (*LW* 36, 19); *WA* 6, 518 (*LW* 36, 44).

[8] *WA* 6, 536 (*LW* 36, 70).

[9] *WA* 6, 541 (*LW* 36, 78); *WA* 6, 567 (*LW* 36, 117); *WA* 6, 563 (*LW* 36, 112); *WA* 6, 547 (*LW* 36, 87).

[10] *WA* 6, 543 (*LW* 36, 82).

[11] *WA* 6, 547 (*LW* 36, 87); *WA* 6, 566 (*LW* 36, 115); *WA* 6, 564 (*LW* 36, 112).

[12] *WA* 6, 566 (*LW* 36, 116); *WA* 6, 543–544 (*LW* 36, 83); *WA* 6, 550 (*LW* 36, 91).

[13] *WA* 6, 521–522 (*LW* 36, 49).

[14] *WA* 6, 542 (*LW* 36, 81).

[15] *WA* 6, 540–541 (*LW* 36, 77–78).

[16] *WA* 6, 527 (*LW* 36, 58–59); *WA* 6, 532–533 (*LW* 36, 66); *WA* 6, 536 (*LW* 36, 70); *WA* 6, 535 (*LW* 36, 69).

[17] *WA* 6, 538 (*LW* 36, 73–74).

[18] *WA* 6, 526–527 (*LW* 36, 57); *WA* 6, 530 (*LW* 36, 63).

[19] *WA* 6, 536 (*LW* 36, 71); *WA* 6, 504 (*LW* 36, 22); *WA* 6, 557 (*LW* 36, 101); *WA* 6, 548 (*LW* 36, 89); *WA* 6, 527 (*LW* 36, 58).

[20] *WA* 6, 553 (*LW* 36, 96); *WA* 6, 525 (*LW* 36, 55); *WA* 6, 537 (*LW* 36, 72); *WA* 6, 536 (*LW* 36, 70); *WA* 6, 504–505 (*LW* 36, 23–24).

[21] *WA* 6, 503 (*LW* 36, 21); *WA* 6, 554–555 (*LW* 36, 98–99; *WA* 6, 559–560 (*LW* 36, 105–106); *WA* 6, 558 (*LW* 36, 103).

[22] *WA* 6, 571 (*LW* 36, 123); *WA* 6, 562 (*LW* 36, 109); *WA* 6, 568 (*LW* 36, 118); *WA* 6, 549 (*LW* 36, 91); *WA* 6, 551 (*LW* 36, 93); *WA* 6, 501 (*LW* 36, 18).

[23] *WA* 6, 533 (*LW* 36, 67); *WA* 6, 507 (*LW* 36, 27–28); *WA* 6, 570–571 (*LW* 36, 122); *WA* 6, 572–573 (*LW* 36, 123–124); *WA* 6, 549 (*LW* 36, 91); *WA* 6, 511 (*LW* 36, 35).

[24] *WA* 6, 523 (*LW* 36, 52); *WA* 6, 512 (*LW* 36, 36); *WA* 6, 533 (*LW* 36, 66); *WA* 6, 510 (*LW* 36, 32).

[25] *WA* 6, 549 (*LW* 36, 90); *WA* 6, 545 (*LW* 36, 85); *WA* 6, 501 (*LW* 36, 18); *WA* 6, 572 (*LW* 36, 124); *WA* 6, 546 (*LW* 36, 86).

[26] *WA* 6, 550 (*LW* 36, 92); *WA* 6, 520 (*LW* 36, 47); *WA* 6, 517 (*LW* 36, 42); *WA* 6, 516 (*LW* 36, 41); *WA* 6, 532 (*LW* 36, 65).

CHAPTER 2. PRIESTHOOD AND MINISTRY (1523)

[1] *WA* 11, 408–416 (*WML* 4, 75–85). Cf. Ivar Asheim (ed.), *Kirche, Mystik, Heiligung und das Natürliche bei Luther* (Göttingen, 1967), pp. 143–155.

[2] *WA* 12, 169–196 (*LW* 40, 7–44); this summary of the Czech situation is based on Ferdinand Hrejsa, *Dejiny krestanství v Ceskoslovensku* (Praha, 1948), IV, 41–61, 93–114, 242–281.

[3] Paul Pietsch in *WA* 12, 163.

[4] *WA* 12, 171 (*LW* 40, 9); *WA* 12, 190 (*LW* 40, 36); cf. Ludwig Pastor, *History of the Popes,* ed. F. I. Antrobus, VI (2nd ed.; St. Louis, 1902), 440.

[5] *WA* 12, 172 (*LW* 40, 10); *WA* 12, 193–194 (*LW* 40, 40–41).

[6] *WA* 12, 194 (*LW* 40, 41).

[7] *WA* 12, 170 (*LW* 40, 8); *WA* 12, 176 (*LW* 40, 16); *WA* 12, 187–188 (*LW* 40, 31–33); *WA* 12, 186 (*LW* 40, 30); *WA* 12, 185 (*LW* 40, 28).

[8] *WA* 12, 169 (*LW* 40, 7–8); *WA* 12, 178 (*LW* 40, 18–19); *WA* 12, 181 (*LW* 40, 23); *WA* 12, 185 (*LW* 40, 29); *WA* 12, 190 (*LW* 40, 35); *WA* 12, 192 (*LW* 40, 38–39).

[9] *WA* 12, 175 (*LW* 40, 14–15); *WA* 12, 196 (*LW* 40, 44).

[10] *WA* 12, 178 (*LW* 40, 18–19); *WA* 12, 179 (*LW* 40, 20).

[11] *WA* 12, 184 (*LW* 40, 26); *WA* 12, 189 (*LW* 40, 34).

[12] *WA* 12, 170 (*LW* 40, 8); *WA* 12, 189 (*LW* 40, 34); *WA* 12, 183 (*LW* 40, 25); *WA* 12, 190 (*LW* 40, 35).

[13] *WA* 12, 171 (*LW* 40, 10); *WA* 12, 186 (*LW* 40, 29).

[14] *WA* 12, 195 (*LW* 40, 42); *WA* 12, 182 (*LW* 40, 24); *WA* 12, 191 (*LW* 40, 37).

[15] *WA* 12, 184 (*LW* 40, 27); *WA* 12, 180 (*LW* 40, 21); *WA* 12, 191 (*LW* 40, 37).

[16] *WA* 12, 171 (*LW* 40, 9); *WA* 12, 181 (*LW* 40, 23); *WA* 12, 173 (*LW* 40, 11); *WA* 12, 192 (*LW* 40, 38); *WA* 12, 193 (*LW* 40, 39).

[17] Cf. Jaroslav Pelikan, *Obedient Rebels* (New York and London, 1964), pp. 123–125.

[18] Cf. Carl S. Mundinger, *Government in the Missouri Synod* (St. Louis, 1947), pp. 213–219.

[19] Cf. Brian A. Gerrish, "Luther on Priesthood and Ministry," *Church History,* XXXIV (1965), 404–422.

CHAPTER 3. MONASTICISM (1523–1524)

[1] See p. 15 above. Cf. *The Springfielder,* XXX–1 (October, 1967,), 3–21.

[2] *The Judgment of Martin Luther on Monastic Vows, WA* 8, 573–669 (*LW* 44, 251–400); Bernhard Lohse, *Mönchtum und Reformation* (Göttingen, 1963), p. 378.

[3] David Knowles, *The Religious Orders in England,* III, *The Tudor Age* (Cambridge, 1959), 203.

[4] *Concerning Rebaptism, WA* 26, 147 (*LW* 40, 231); *WA TR* 2, 447; *Church Postil, WA* 10–I–1, 21; Kenneth Scott Latourette, *A History of the Expansion of Christianity* (7 vols.; New York, 1937–1945), II, 17; III, 26.

[5] See Armas K. E. Holmio, *The Lutheran Reformation and the Jews* (Hancock, Mich., 1949); Luther to Bernard, a baptized Jew, June (?), 1523, *Wa Br* 3, 102; cf. *StL* 20, 1807; Roland H. Bainton, *Here I Stand. A Life of Martin Luther* (New York, 1950), p. 379.

[6] *Military Sermon Against the Turk, WA* 30–II, 194–195.

[7] See Werner Elert, *The Structure of Lutheranism,* tr. Walter A. Hansen (St. Louis, 1962), pp. 385–402.

[8] Cf. F. Dean Lueking, *Mission in the Making* (St. Louis, 1964), esp. pp. 24–44.

[9] Yves M.-J. Congar, "Aspects ecclésiologiques de la querelle entre mendiants et séculiers dans la seconde moitié du XIII° siècle et le début du XIV°," *Archives d'histoire doctrinale et littéraire du moyen age*, 28 (1961), 35–151.

[10] *The Sermon on the Mount, WA* 32, 307 (*LW* 21, 12–13); *WA* 32, 301 (*LW* 21, 6); *WA* 32, 300 (*LW* 21, 4); in this connection cf. Jaroslav Pelikan, *The Preaching of Chrysostom* (Philadelphia, 1967), esp. pp. 28–34.

[11] *To the Christian Nobility of the German Nation Concerning the Reform of the Christian Estate, WA* 6, 450–451 (*LW* 44, 190); Joan M. Hussey, *The Byzantine World* (New York, 1961), p. 139.

[12] *To the Christian Nobility, WA* 6, 450 (*LW* 44, 190); Luther to Spalatin, September 25, 1522, *WA Br* 2, 604; Luther to Leisnig, January 29, 1523, *WA Br* 3, 23.

[13] *Ordinance of a Common Chest, Preface, WA* 12, 11–12 (*LW* 45, 169–170).

[14] *WA* 12, 12 (*LW* 45, 171).

[15] *WA* 12, 12–13 (*LW* 45, 171–172).

[16] *WA* 12, 14 (*LW* 45, 173); *WA* 12, 11–12 (*LW* 45, 170).

[17] *WA* 12, 13–15 (*LW* 45, 172–176).

[18] Luther to Frederick of Saxony, August 11, 1523, *WA Br* 3, 125; Luther to Frederick of Saxony, August 19, 1523, *WA Br* 3, 128–129; Luther to Spalatin, November 24, 1524, *WA Br* 3, 390–391.

[19] Luther to Lang, January 22, 1525, *WA Br* 3, 427; Luther to John of Saxony, September 16, 1527, *WA Br* 4, 248; *Preface to Book of Vagabonds, WA* 26, 639; *Preface to Sermon on Almsgiving, WA* 38, 72–74.

[20] Sermon on December 26, 1523, *WA* 12, 693, 27–38.

[21] Cf. the bibliographical references in *LW* 45, 344–345.

[22] *On Monastic Vows, WA* 8, 614–615 (*LW* 44, 312–313); *WA* 8, 641 (*LW* 44, 355).

[23] *To the Councilmen of Germany, WA* 15, 47 (*LW* 45, 371); *WA* 15, 51 (*LW* 45, 351); *WA* 15, 30 (*LW* 45, 350); *WA* 15, 33 (*LW* 45, 354); *WA* 15, 50–51 (*LW* 45, 375).

[24] *WA* 15, 47 (*LW* 45, 371); *WA* 15, 51 (*LW* 45, 375); *StL* 22, 950–969; *WA* 8, 655 (*LW* 44, 378).

[25] *WA* 15, 31 (*LW* 45, 351–352); *WA* 15, 52 (*LW* 45, 377); cf. *Obedient Rebels,* pp. 183 ff.

[26] *WA* 15, 36 (*LW* 45, 358); *WA* 15, 38 (*LW* 45, 360).

[27] *WA* 15, 28 (*LW* 45, 348); *WA* 15, 30 (*LW* 45, 351); *WA* 15, 47–48 (*LW* 45, 371).

[28] *WA* 15, 36 (*LW* 45, 358); *WA* 15, 42 (*LW* 45, 365–366).

[29] *WA* 15, 43–44 (*LW* 45, 367); *WA* 15, 35 (*LW* 45, 356–357).

[30] *WA* 15, 33 (*LW* 45, 354); *WA* 15, 44–45 (*LW* 45, 368); *WA* 15, 48 (*LW* 45, 372).

CHAPTER 4. THE PROBLEMS OF INFANT BAPTISM (1527–1528).

[1] Adolf Harnack, *History of Dogma,* tr. Neil Buchanan (New York, 1961), VII, 248, 251. Cf. Carl S. Meyer (ed.), *Luther for an Ecumenical Age* (St. Louis, 1967), pp. 200–218.

[2] *Concerning Rebaptism, WA* 26, 172 (*LW* 40, 260).

[3] *WA* 26, 154 (*LW* 40, 239); *WA* 26, 156 (*LW* 40, 241–242).

[4] *WA* 26, 156, 10 (*LW* 40, 242); *Tertullian's Homily on Baptism,* ed. Ernest Evans (London, 1964), xviii, pp. 36–41, and the editor's comments, pp. 101–106; *The Order of Baptism, WA* 12, 45 (*LW* 53, 98–99).

[5] *WA* 26, 144–145 (*LW* 40, 229); Wilhelm Pauck, *The Heritage of the Reformation* (2nd ed.; Glencoe, Ill., 1961), pp. 19–28; *WA* 26, 154 (*LW* 40, 240); *WA* 26, 157–158 (*LW* 40, 244).

[6] *WA* 26, 163 (*LW* 40, 250); *Confession Concerning Christ's Supper, WA* 26, 491 (*LW* 37, 354); *WA* 26, 159 (*LW* 40, 246).

[7] *Confession Concerning Christ's Supper, WA* 26, 321 (*LW* 37, 210); *WA* 26, 149–150 (*LW* 40, 234–235).

[8] *WA* 26, 163 (*LW* 40, 250); Brian A. Gerrish, *Grace and*

Reason. A Study in the Theology of Luther (Oxford, 1962), esp. pp. 138–152.

[9] *WA* 26, 150–151 (*LW* 40, 235–236).

[10] *WA* 26, 151–152 (*LW* 40, 236–237); *WA* 26, 163 (*LW* 40, 251); *WA* 26, 153 (*LW* 40, 239).

[11] Small Catechism, IV, 11, *Bek.* 516 (*BC* 349).

[12] *Confession Concerning Christ's Supper, WA* 26, 462 (*LW* 37, 317); *WA* 26, 146–147 (*LW* 40, 231); *WA* 26, 148 (*LW* 40, 233).

[13] *WA* 26, 147–148 (*LW* 40, 232–233); *WA* 26, 169 (*LW* 40, 257).

[14] *WA* 26, 167–169 (*LW* 40, 255–257); *WA* 26, 153 (*LW* 40, 238).

[15] *WA* 26, 168 (*LW* 40, 256); Large Catechism, IV, 50, *Bek.* 701 (*BC* 443).

[16] *WA* 26, 155 (*LW* 40, 241); *WA* 26, 167 (*LW* 40, 255); *WA* 26, 166 (*LW* 40, 254); *WA* 26, 159 (*LW* 40, 245); *WA* 26, 168 (*LW* 40, 256).

[17] *Lectures on Galatians, WA* 40–I, 589 (*LW* 26, 387).

[18] *WA* 26, 164 (*LW* 40, 252); *WA* 26, 158 (*LW* 40, 245); *WA* 26, 153 (*LW* 40, 239); *WA* 26, 155 (*LW* 40, 240–241).

[19] *WA* 26, 158 (*LW* 40, 244); *WA* 26, 164 (*LW* 40, 252); *WA* 26, 169 (*LW* 40, 257).

[20] *WA* 26, 168 (*LW* 40, 256).

[21] Cf. John S. Oyer, *Lutheran Reformers Against Anabaptists* (The Hague, 1964) on the whole problem.

[22] See also pp. 119–121 ff.

[23] Sermon on July 25, 1522, *WA* 10–III, 239.

CHAPTER 5.   CHURCH LAW AND DIVINE LAW
(1530–1531).

[1] *An Account of the Burning of the Decretals of the Antichrist, WA* 7, 184, 186; *Why the Books of the Pope and His Disciples Were Burned by Doctor Martin Luther, WA* 7, 168 (*LW* 31, 384); *Defense and Explanation of All the Articles of Dr. Martin Luther, WA* 7, 432 (*LW* 32, 83). Cf. Alfons

M. Stickler (ed.), *Collectanea Stephan Kuttner,* I (Rome, 1967), pp. 367–388.

[2] *On Marriage Matters, WA* 30–III, 206, 208 (*LW* 46, 267–268.

[3] Apology of the Augsburg Confession, Preface, 11, *Bek.* 143 (*BC* 99).

[4] XXIII, 57, *Bek.* 344 (*BC* 247); IV, 362, *Bek.* 228 (*BC* 162).

[5] XI, 7, *Bek.* 251 (*BC* 181); XXI, 41, *Bek.* 326 (*BC* 235); Preface, 17, *Bek.* 144 (*BC* 99); XII, 3, *Bek.* 253 (*BC* 183); IV, 288, *Bek.* 217 (*BC* 151); IV, 380, *Bek.* 231 (*BC* 165).

[6] IV, 269, *Bek.* 214 (*BC* 147); IV, 16, *Bek.* 162 (*BC* 109); XXVII, 52, *Bek.* 392 (*BC* 278); XI, 9, *Bek.* 252 (*BC* 182); XV, 27, *Bek.* 302 (*BC* 219).

[7] For a full catalogue and an analysis of these quotations, see my essay referred to in note 1 above.

[8] VII, 10, *Bek.* 235–236 (*BC* 170).

[9] XV, 38–39, *Bek.* 304 (*BC* 220).

[10] XVI, 3, *Bek.* 308 (*BC* 223); XIII, 12, *Bek.* 294 (*BC* 212); XIV, 1–2, *Bek.* 286–287 (*BC* 214).

[11] XV, 49, *Bek.* 306 (*BC* 221–222).

[12] XII, 145, *Bek.* 283 (*BC* 205).

[13] XXVII, 30, *Bek.* 387 (*BC* 274); XV, 10, *Bek.* 298 (*BC* 216); IV, 265, *Bek.* 213 (*BC* 146); IV, 10–11, *Bek.* 161 (*BC* 108); VII, 32, *Bek.* 242 (*BC* 174); XII, 120–121, *Bek.* 277 (*BC* 200); XII, 167, *Bek.* 288 (*BC* 208–209).

[14] XXVII, 20, *Bek.* 383 (*BC* 272); VII, 38, *Bek.* 244 (*BC* 176); VII, 46, *Bek.* 246 (*BC* 177).

[15] XXIII, 3, *Bek.* 333 (*BC* 239); XXIII, 7, 9, *Bek.* 335 (*BC* 240); XXIII, 23–24, *Bek.* 339 (*BC* 242–243).

[16] XV, 44, *Bek.* 205 (*BC* 221); XXIV, 49–50, *Bek.* 364 (*BC* 258–259); XXIV, 1, *Bek.* 349 (*BC* 249); XV, 41, *Bek.* 305 (*BC* 220).

[17] IV, 22, *Bek.* 164 (*BC* 110); VII, 33–34, *Bek.* 242–243 (*BC* 174–175); XXIII, 49, *Bek.* 343 (*BC* 246); XV, 13, *Bek.* 299 (*BC* 216).

CHAPTER 6. The Sacramental System (1537)

[1] *History of Dogma,* VII, 216. Cf. Heino A. Kadai (ed.), *Accents in Luther's Theology* (St. Louis, 1967), pp. 124–147.

[2] Augsburg Confession, V, 1, *Bek.* 58 (*BC* 31).

[3] Augsburg Confession, XIII, *Bek.* 68 (*BC* 36).

[4] Elector John Frederick to Luther and his colleagues, December 11, 1536, *WA Br* 7, 613.

[5] Smalcald Articles, Part III, Article VI, *Bek.* 449 (*BC* 310).

[6] *Sermons on the Gospel of St. John, WA* 46, 582 (*LW* 22, 54).

[7] *Lectures on Romans, WA* 56, 426 (English translation by Wilhelm Pauck [Philadelphia, 1961], p. 301); *Lectures on Genesis, WA* 42, 241 (*LW* 1, 327).

[8] *Lectures on Galatians, WA* 40–I, 528 (*LW* 26, 344–345).

[9] *Prefaces to the New Testament, WA DB* 6, 3 (*LW* 35, 358).

[10] Cf. Jaroslav Pelikan, *Luther the Expositor* (St. Louis, 1959), pp. 48–70.

[11] Cf. pp. 93–96 above.

[12] Large Catechism, IV, 28–29, *Bek.* 696 (*BC* 440).

[13] See also pp. 37–43 on the problem of continuity.

[14] See also pp. 24–26.

[15] Cf. *Obedient Rebels,* pp. 136–146.

[16] *The Adoration of the Sacrament, WA* 11, 441 (*LW* 36, 288); *Luther the Expositor,* pp. 237–254.

[17] *Against the Heavenly Prophets, WA* 18, 197 (*LW* 40, 207–208.

[18] *The Blessed Sacrament of the Holy and True Body of Christ, and the Brotherhoods, WA* 2, 743 (*LW* 35, 50–51).

[19] *The Sermon on the Mount, WA* 32, 404, 463 (*LW* 21, 126, 198).

[20] Cf. pp. 28–29 above; Apology, XIII, 4, *Bek.* 292 (*BC* 211).

[21] *The Sacrament of Penance, WA* 2, 717 (*LW* 35, 13).

[22] Cf. G. A. Westberg, "Private Confession in the Lutheran Church," *Augustana Quarterly*, XXIV, 138–162.

[23] *The Sacrament of Penance, WA* 2, 719 (*LW* 35, 17).

[24] *Concerning the Ministry, WA* 12, 184 (*LW* 40, 27).

[25] Cf. Pauck, *The Heritage of the Reformation*, pp. 29–59.

[26] *The German Mass and Order of Service, WA* 19, 75 (*LW* 53, 64); *The Sermon on the Mount, WA* 32, 484 (*LW* 21, 223).

[27] *Commentary on Psalm 90, WA* 40–III, 506–507 (*LW* 13, 89–90).

EPILOGUE: Spirit in Structure

[1] See p. 16, pp. 93–94, and p. 73 above.

[2] Cf. Jaroslav Pelikan, "Adolf von Harnack on Luther" in Jaroslav Pelikan (ed.), *Interpreters of Luther* (Philadelphia, 1968) p. 262; and "Jozef Miloslav Hurban: A Study in Historicism" in Jerald C. Brauer (ed.), *The Impact of the Church upon its Culture* (Chicago, 1968), p. 348.

[3] See the classic essay of Karl Holl, "Martin Luther on Luther," *Interpreters of Luther*, pp. 9–34.

[4] Paul Tillich, *Systematic Theology* (3 vols. in one; New York and Chicago, 1967), III, 250.

[5] *That These Words of Christ, "This Is My Body," etc., Still Stand Firm Against the Fanatics, WA* 23, 151 (*LW* 37, 68–69).